FROM
DARKNESS
TO
LIGHT

GOD IS OUR ONLY REFUGE

DENIS IVIC

PAGE PUBLISHING, INC.
Conneaut Lake, PA

First originally published by Page Publishing 2021

Some names in the book have been changed
for easier pronunciation in English.
All scriptures are taken from the King
James Version of the Bible.
Credits:
Translated from Serbian to English
by Jasmina Dinic-Ciric
Proofread by Gabriella Ivic
Cover photo by Denis Ivic and Ljubodrag Cirkovic
Photography by Denis Ivic and Gabriella Ivic

ISBN 978-1-6624-3234-7 (pbk)
ISBN 978-1-6624-3235-4 (digital)

Printed in the United States of America

ACKNOWLEDGMENTS

I would like to thank my mother for her sacrifice. She saved me from my father's abuse many times. She put herself in danger to protect me from my father. If she were alive today, she would be very happy to read this book. I was really blessed with a wonderful mother.

I am thankful for the friendship of Dragan Stanic. He helped me very much during the difficult times in my life. Thank you, Dragan, for everything.

Another person I need to thank is Ljubodrag Cirkovic (Cira as everybody calls him) for introducing me to the Lord. I learned a lot about God through him.

I have to mention my pastor David Adamovic and his wife Lilja from Serbia. David has always been very patient with me. He taught me about God every day before my baptism, and I am still learning from him. His wife Lilja has been a great support for me as well.

Many thanks to my mother-in-law. She was a great woman. She loved me as if I were her own son. I learned a lot of things from her too. Although we had a language barrier, we were able to talk and spent some good time together. She helped me with everything in Hungary, including translation, filling out forms, and talking to officials. I am glad to have known her.

Zoran and Dragana have been very important to me as well. They were very supportive in Hungary when I was corresponding with Gabriella, my future wife, on the Internet. Without Zoran's translation, I wouldn't have been able to communicate with Gabriella.

I would like to thank the translator of this book, Jasmina Ciric Dinic. She has done a great job of translating my words and thoughts from Serbian into English.

Finally, special thanks to my sweetheart, Gabriella. It has been a real privilege to share everything with her in life. She has always been there for me. When I have pain, she feels my pain. When I smile, she smiles too. I cannot thank her enough for these twenty years of heaven on earth. These twenty years have been very little time for me. I would like to live with her forever and ever.

They say that the fate of a man is predetermined by the place where he was born. This is where my story begins.

My name is Denis Ivic, and I was born on April 18, 1960, in Smederevo, Serbia. Originally, my father came from Kosovo and my mother from Croatia. At that time, Serbia was part of Yugoslavia. Somewhere else in the world, this would have been just a minor detail, but in multinational Yugoslavia, this was a significant fact.

My mother was born into a wealthy family. Her father was a merchant who sold clothes and shoes. Prior to World War II, my mother's grandfather had sailed to the United States of America. Many years later, I followed in his footsteps. My father had three sisters and two brothers. They were poor and honest people who barely made ends meet.

During World War II, the Italian occupation authorities confiscated all properties from my mother's father, my grandfather. They did this because my grandfather refused to cooperate. He did not want to be involved in the turbulent political situation. He just wanted to take care of his family. Ironically, he was falsely accused of cooperating with the Italians and shot by the Partisans. Hard times came for the family. They were left without the head of the family and all their properties. My mother just turned twelve. She had two sisters and five brothers. They had no money, so they started working to earn a living. My mother got a job as a maid. She did all the work in and around the house. She also worked in the barn, taking care of the animals, and slept there too. People were mocking her for not having anything at all. Life was very cruel to my mother, her sisters, and her brothers at the time.

During her childhood, my mom was learning life lessons the hard way. The will to live, the determination to pick up the pieces, and starting all over again became her goals. Later, she became a caring mother who always protected and encouraged her children. Her care for us was never less than pure love and kindness. She was the best and most beautiful mother in the world for me. If there were Medals of Bravery for mothers, my mother would have been given one bigger than the Empire State Building.

I do not know much about my father's childhood. All I know is that he was born in a large family in Kosovo. They worked hard, struggling to get by.

When World War II broke out, my father joined the Partisans, the resistance movement. He was a courier. His duty was to collect and carry messages for the Partisans behind enemy lines. It was a very dangerous job. At the end of the war, he was promoted to an officer for his bravery. He received a pistol as a reward from Vice President Aleksandar Rankovic. The pistol was a Czechoslovakian Zbrojevka, bearing the inscription "for distinguished service in World War II." After the war, my father was engaged in demining operations in Zadar. Zadar is a Croatian city on the Adriatic Sea. My father met my mother there. It was love at first sight. The year was 1950. My mother's family did not like that she was seeing someone of a different ethnic group, but she did not care. My father and mother rushed to get married to obey the social norms of the time.

This is a photo of my parents
on their wedding day.

At that time, my mother worked for a wealthy woman who helped my parents make a nice wedding reception. They began their married life together in Zadar. Soon after the wedding, when my father finished the work he had come to do, my parents decided to move to Kosovo, my father's birthplace. It was Lajcici, a little village near the town of Gnjilan. The villagers lived without water or electricity there. In addition to poor living conditions, my mother was burdened with my father's disrespectful family. They did not like her because she was Croatian. Although ethnically close, Yugoslav people were of different cultural and religious backgrounds as well as traditional practices. These differences affected my parents' marriage. My mother tried in vain to be accepted by the family.

My parents had a baby boy, my eldest brother Marijan, in 1952. After a series of attempts to have a successful life in Kosovo, they decided to move and start a new life elsewhere. Their choice was to move to Smederevo. Smederevo was one of the major cities in Serbia with a developing industry at that time and a growing number of job openings in the Smederevo steel plant.

My parents encountered problems from the start. With a baby and little money, it was difficult for them to find a decent place to live. They did not know anyone in the new place, so they had to rely solely on their own strengths and abilities. My father got a job as a smelter in the steel plant. It was hard work because almost everything was done manually.

My mother also tried to earn some money by cleaning the homes of wealthy local people. My parents rented a house from a Romani woman. It was actually a shabby, moldy smelling room with no furniture and carpet at all. According to my mother, they had to improvise. There were no pillows, so they placed pans and rugs under their heads. They made blankets and mattresses from coats, and each time they changed position, their sleep was disturbed by the creaking of metal pans on the concrete floor.

After the war was over, some of the prisoners of war decided not to return to their countries and remained in Yugoslavia. Therefore, some Germans, Italians, and Bulgarians settled down in Smederevo. At first, the authorities looked at them with suspicion. This was the reason why my father, besides working as a smelter and a participant in the Partisan movement during the war, also got hired by security to help prevent diversions. Soon after, my parents got an apartment from the plant. The apartment was by "the beautiful blue Danube," as Johann Strauss once said. My father's earnings were slightly better, and a period of happiness and well-being followed. In 1954, my sister Nance was born then Rick in 1956. After Rick, my sister Gina came to this world in 1958, and finally, I arrived in 1960. My father was not happy that my mother was pregnant with me. He became violent and started beating my mom. Because of the stress and frequent beating, my mother gave birth to me prematurely. She brought me into the world in the seventh month of pregnancy. The doctors said I would not survive. I weighed only 3.3 pounds. Now I know that God wanted me to live for a definite purpose.

As time went on, my father was becoming worse and worse. He drank a lot every day, had sex with other women, and maltreated my mother. On one occasion, he brought a prostitute over to our apartment and had sex with her while my mother was locked in the pantry. He was unbearable. He beat our mother and did not care about us at all. Some people who were jealous of my father's good job and salary encouraged him to drink and be with prostitutes. The same envious men reported him to the management for neglecting his duties, hinting that he was unworthy of this job. They came up with malicious stories, and he got fired. We were desperate. He let alcoholism take over his life, and his condition was such that he could no longer work. Taking into account his war merits and qualifying years, he was entitled to a minimum pension for early retirement. As a participant in the Partisan movement during the war, he was also entitled to a veteran's pension, which could have been a significant income for our family, but he refused it. As an act of protest, he did not want to receive the same pension as those whose participation in the war was suspicious and questionable.

It seemed as if a curse had been placed on our family. Persuaded by his alcoholic friends, my father was about to move us to the outskirts of the city under the pretext that we could raise pigs, chickens, and other animals there. At that time, we lived in a nice, comfortable apartment in a great location, and I often played with Lassie, a yellowish dog. She actually belonged to all the children in the neighborhood, but Marijan, my oldest brother, often brought her to our apartment, and I took care of her. Playing with Lassie was the utmost joy for me. I could not imagine that we would move soon and that I would never see my Lassie again. It struck me hard.

Moving a family with five children into a small apartment on the outskirts of the city was an irrational decision. My mother objected, but my father did not care much about what she thought. It is undoubtedly always a challenge to accept a lower standard of living. My mom and we, the little ones, were desperate, but my father's friends felt content to have another alcoholic in their group of idlers. He enjoyed hanging out with scumbags. He lost his reputation, and alcohol became his sole consolation. At the end of June, he sold our apartment for a bottle of brandy. My mother did not even know about it. My father was very obstinate and self-willed and never asked his wife for an opinion.

We were left homeless. My mother could not do anything but give in and agree to move. We returned to our father's hometown Lajcici, a little village near the town of Gnjilan in Kosovo. There was still no water or electricity there. Living with no electricity was really difficult. We had to walk miles to fetch water from the spring as the village stream was far away. The narrow path to the spring led through a dense forest. The forest was big and just as dark on a sunny day as in the moonlight. At that time, I was only four years old. I went to the spring with my mother, sisters Nance and Gina, or with some of my neighbors.

The village of Lajcici was a small one. It consisted of about forty to fifty houses scattered a fair distance from one another. It was surrounded by the forest. On a few occasions, wolves came into the village at night, attacking the barns and killing the sheep, goats, and cows. We were scared of the wolves and often could not sleep at night, but eventually, we got used to it.

My father had a strange uncle named Hudson. He was both mentally ill and unable to speak. He could only make some incomprehensible sounds. One night, he went star hunting. He took his rifle, pointed it up at the dark sky, and fired it. He wanted to shoot a star so badly. Somehow, at the very moment, there was a falling star, and Hudson thought he had shot a star. Feeling satisfied, he placed his rifle on his shoulder and went straight home to sleep. The next night, he went star hunting again. It was a very bright night with a full moon. He pointed the rifle up at the sky and fired many times. No stars fell. Frustrated and angry, he continued to fire. None of the family members could not sleep because of the noise. They went out and asked him to stop shooting. This made him even angrier, so he aimed at them. They knew that Uncle Hudson was not joking. They panicked and immediately threw themselves down on the ground, looking for cover. He fired again. Thank God no one was hurt.

That episode had a happy ending, but Hudson had a lot more strange adventures. At the end of July, a combine arrived at the village to harvest the wheat fields. After the harvest, it collected leftover crops from the fields for the villagers to feed their cattle during the winter. Once again, Hudson was the main character in a little drama on that summer day. The combine driver was doing the work when suddenly he seemed to see a sheep lying in the middle of the wheat field, blocking the way. He stopped the engine, got off the combine, and tried to scare the sheep away. As he got closer, he realized that it was not a sheep lying in the field but a man wrapped in two sheepskin coats. It was Uncle Hudson who was sleeping there. The combine driver woke him up. Hudson was all sweating under the sheepskin coats. He got angry and slapped the man in the face twice. The driver was confused as he did not know Hudson and anything about his mental state. He tried to explain to Hudson that he could have gotten hurt by the combine. It seemed Hudson understood what the man told him. He went home, feeling happy that he had not gotten hurt. Rarely could anyone understand Hudson. He was stubbornly convinced he was always right. Therefore, those who knew him well did not pay attention to him. They knew he was difficult and narrow-minded, so they avoided provoking him.

It is hard when you are surrounded on every side by danger—wolves from the forest and Uncle

Hudson at home. It was difficult to say what was more dangerous. Everything seemed to be a better option for my mother than living under constant fear. After a year of hard life in Lajcici in Kosovo, my mother managed to persuade my father to return to Smederevo and start over.

We returned to Smederevo in August 1965. We left everything in Lajcici. We did not have anything again—not even a place to live in. One man offered us his shed to stay in until we got back on our feet. He also gave us some clothes, mattresses, quilts, and bedsheets. The shed had been used for storing firewood and coal for the winter. There were numerous holes in the walls through which the wind was blowing in. The shed was cold and smelled of coal, wood, mold, and mildew. It took us a lot of time to get used to living there. Although we lived in this cold shed, we were happy because we were not in Lajcici any longer. During the day, our parents were out at work, and we, little children, stayed home alone. There were five of us, and we spent the days locked in the shed, waiting for our parents to return and bring us some food. The sun shyly peeked through the cracks in the walls, slightly illuminating the interior of the dark shed. While our parents were at work, we were impatiently waiting for them. When they got home, we would ravenously fall on the food placed before us. A full stomach made for a happy heart.

Locked in the shed and dressed in scruffy old clothes, we probably looked strange to the children in the neighborhood. They came closer to our shed, staring at us and mocking us. But we were happy because we saw some new faces. If we could have gone out to play with those kids, we would have been in seventh heaven.

We felt miserable and humiliated because of our living conditions. Even the orphans in state institutions lived in better conditions. We had both parents but lived locked in the shed. My mother fought for us with all her strength while my father was only interested in drinking, which I could not understand. The shed was made of wooden boards. It smelled of the remains of coal and rotted wood, and the cracks in the walls let the cold air in, so we could not sleep at night. Nevertheless, I was grateful to the Lord that we had at least this shed because it was better than living under the open sky.

One good man, named Milan, felt pity for us and offered to let us move to his pigsty. It was about 14 feet long, 14 feet wide, and 5 feet high. Milan used to keep pigs in it. It smelled awful from the pigs. When it rained, the roof leaked, so not only we but also our beds got wet. About fifty feet away from our shack, there was a large round pit, about twenty-one feet across and seven feet deep that everyone used for a garbage dump. It was filled with concrete, rotten food, dead animals, etc. It's hard to say if the smell was worse in there or in our pigsty. There was no heat or stove in the sty, so we could not dry our clothes or make some soup to keep us warm. That was the reason why we often got sick. My father continued to drink every day, and we did not have enough food.

We spent the whole winter there. When we got an old stove, we managed to keep our home at least a little warm. The days dragged on monotonously. Every day was just like the day before. My father came home drunk almost every day.

Trying to escape from our drunken father and the problems he brought with him, my older brothers and sister hid in the neighborhood. These were nice people who let them stay with them. While they stayed there for days, my sister Gina, my mother, and I stayed at home. My father never loved me. I could feel it. But I could not understand how a father could not love his child. Surprisingly, he never beat Gina, but he beat me very often and a lot. When my father returned home drunk, he liked to sing. His singing was a warning signal for me. As soon as I heard him singing, I would hide under the bed. It was very cold lying on the ground under the bed. It was winter, and there were two feet of snow outside. Even today, I do not know whether I was shivering with cold or from the fear of my father. One night, my father came home. He knew that I was under the bed because there was no other place to hide, and he grabbed me with his hands. I was scared for my life. I grabbed one of the legs of the bed, trying to avoid being beaten. I trembled with fear and started to cry but did not give up. I held on to the leg of the bed with all my strength. I was ready to stay forever under the bed on the cold ground in order not to have to look at my father's mad face. My mother came to help me, but my father pushed her into the corner. There was no way out for me. He grabbed me again and started beating mercilessly. He slapped me in the face then hit me in the stomach and kicked me in the legs. He beat the hell out of me. I thought he would kill me. He hit me again and again until I could no longer sustain the pain, so my legs went numb, my body shut down, and I fell to the ground. My mother rose to her feet and pushed him away from me. He stumbled and fell. Shocked and confused that he was on the ground, he got back up, grabbed a gun pointing at our legs, and started shooting. My mother, Gina, and I jumped to our feet and ran out. Being scared of the gunshots, I did not even feel my pain anymore. I thought I would go deaf from those gunshots.

It was snowing outside. We were barefoot with barely any clothes on. My feet felt the wet snow. The cold was creeping into our toes, but we were running away, trying to save our lives. We ran into our neighbors' yard and hid in their outhouse. It was made from wood boards, smelled bad, and was cold just like outside. The wind was blowing snow inside under the door. My mother gathered us in her arms and put our feet on hers, trying to keep our feet warm. The temperature outside was 10 degrees Fahrenheit. While we were shivering with cold, my father was at home sitting by the hot stove. We could not ask our neighbors for help because they were afraid of my father's reaction. I do not remember how long we stayed there, but it seemed like an eternity. Since we were dressed only in thin, tattered pajamas, the cold gradually made us feel weak and fatigued.

Salvation came quite suddenly. Our neighbor Kosara appeared at the outhouse door. She did not know we were there, so she got scared to death of us. When she pulled herself together and recognized us, she invited us to her house, which was both kind and brave of her. Oh, you cannot imagine how surprised and excited we were. Being frozen, we could hardly walk. So when we entered Kosara's warm home, we did not care about the food offered or anything else. We were so tired that we could not even worry that our father would find us. We fell asleep right away.

The night passed peacefully, and we returned home in the morning. My mother did not want to make trouble for Kosara. We were grateful to her. We agreed not to tell my father where we had spent the night. The next day, my father acted as if nothing had happened. It was his way to show remorse. When he was sober, he was not violent. Unfortunately, he was more often a bully and a drunk. My mother saw no way out of this situation. Her relatives were far away in Croatia, and she could not hope to get any help from them. Furthermore, divorces were very rare at that time. So she accepted the things as they were, stayed with her husband, and we all suffered. The only people from whom we could expect some help were our neighbors, but they were not willing to help us. They were afraid of my father's reaction and did not want to have issues with him. When my father was drunk, he indeed looked as if possessed by demons. I could not understand them. I would always help anyone and take them under my protection.

It is human nature to suppress bad memories. So I tried to calm my mind and forget the past traumatic experiences. I just wanted our problems to end so that we could have a normal life. It was a little boy's dream who loved his life endlessly, trying to forget the horror he was living. Unfortunately, the horror was inextricably intertwined with our lives. My father was a pliable man, and he had a weak character. He trusted some people and believed in their friendships, but they spurred him on to vices and bad decisions while deceiving him into the belief that he was leading the best possible kind of life. His only way out of the mess in his life was brandy. He drank when he was sad, he drank when he was happy, and he drank when things did not go as he had expected. All in all, he drank day after day.

The poorer we became, the more domestic violence we endured. My father was dissatisfied because he had five children, and he blamed us for everything. What else could I say? If it had been up to me, I would have never chosen such a man to be my father. When I look back on my life, it seems to me that often nothing made sense and that my world often turned upside down, but I always fought till my last breath, and I never lost hope. Our father abused us while hunger tortured us.

Once, when I was about six years old, I found an end piece of bread in the pantry. We kept bread in one of the drawers, as we did not have any other place for it. I remember the bread was so stale and hard that nobody wanted it. In my home country, they would say, "It is so hard that you could knock a nail into a piece of wood with it." I was very hungry, and no matter how hard it was, I was bound and determined to eat it. I started to eat it. First, I softened the inside of the bread with my tongue. Then I took one bite, moved it around in my mouth, slightly moistening it with saliva. Then I took another bite, and it went down to my stomach, scratching my throat. Still, this was not enough to suffice my hunger. A much more difficult job was waiting for me. I had to defeat the bread crust. My teeth were weak, my mouth was dry, but I did not give up. I kept biting it from all sides. A lot of time and persistence paid off. Bit by bit, the pieces of hard bread were going down to my stomach. It was a very painful experience, but I was thrilled when I finished. If only I had had a cooked meal along with it.

I have saved this photo by chance. I am the first on the right, my brother Rick is standing next to me, and my friends Nile and Stephen are to the left. I was three or four years old. I do not remember where the photo was taken. We used to have a lot more photos, but many of them got lost as we often moved. If I had all of them, I could recall more of my boyhood memories and moments. Pictures are not only worth a thousand words but also the precious memories embedded into them. For this reason, this photo is so valuable and dear to me as the only one that has remained from my childhood.

I believe a true friend is someone who listens to understand your thoughts and feelings and accepts you for who you are. Truly great friends are the ones who are always there for you, who help you through the hard times, catch you when you stumble, and believe in you when you have ceased to believe in yourself. They say that innocent children make the best friends. My special friend was Bob. Bob was about a year younger than I was. He lived with his parents and sister nearby. They were a very nice family. I learned from them that parents should talk to their children like friends do. Bob's father Paul was completely opposite of my father. His mother Mila was a kind woman. I could not believe that such a happy family existed. They treated me so nicely as if I were their son. It did not matter to them that I came from a poor family and had an abusive father. Some parents did not let their children play with me, but Bob's parents let the two of us play every day.

We would play for hours, and at lunchtime, Bob's mother would call him, and we would stop playing. Bob would go to his home, and I would drag myself home with an empty stomach. Then suddenly, I heard Bob's mother calling me. She invited me to have lunch with them. She was a wise woman. She knew the situation in my family—that my father was an alcoholic and that there was never enough food in the house. She also did not want me to feel uncomfortable, so she always called me on the pretext of having to tell me something. I was ashamed. I would say that I had enough to eat at home, but she was persistent. She would take me by the hand as if I were her son and lead me to the table. Sitting at the table, I was embarrassed and kept looking down.

I was wondering whether my mother and sister had anything to eat while I was sitting there at the full table. I could not have been happy if they had been starving at home that day. Bob's mother placed a bowl of soup on the table, and we started to eat. The soup with fine noodles and lots of veggies just melted in my mouth. It was out of this world! After the soup came the second course. I hesitated, but Bob's family made me feel comfortable. They said that they were glad I was having lunch with them. After lunch, Bob was sent to his afternoon nap, and I went home. It was unthinkable to me how Bob could sleep during the day. Because of my father, I could neither sleep at night nor in the afternoon. Bob was a very good friend, and he shared his toys with me because I did not have any. We enjoyed playing together. I was proud of Bob and our friendship. That day on my way home, I could not imagine what an unpleasant surprise was waiting for me.

Mark, a boy in the neighborhood who was seven or eight years older, told my alcoholic father that I had kicked his ball, which then rolled down the slope and disappeared. It was a complete lie. I did not know why Mark had made this up. That day I had spent playing with Bob as usual, and I had seen neither Mark nor his ball. But my father did not want to hear the truth. He had already made up his mind before even hearing my side of the story.

My father had a walking stick to lean on because of the pain in his legs. He told me to come to him. I knew what was going to happen. I knew that I would get beaten up, but I had no option but to comply. He grabbed me by the arm and started beating me with the stick. He beat me all over my body. He hit me several times on the back, in the thighs, and under my knees. Tears were pouring out of my eyes due to the severe pain. I thought I was going to die. He hit me again and again until I fell to the ground. Then he stopped. He might have thought that he had gone too far and that someone would report him to the police. Then he ran away in an unknown direction. He left me lying on the ground. Our neighbors had been watching all this indifferently, and nobody tried to help me. I was lying there like a wounded bird fighting for life. Someone must have told my mother, so she came running to rescue me. She took me home and put me to bed. I had bruises all over my body and a high fever. I felt such immense pain that I could barely lie in bed. In my mind, there was only the image of my father, a soulless beast. I wanted to run away from him, from home and never return. When my mother went to the pharmacy to get some medicine for me, I sneaked out of the house. I did not have a clear plan. I just wanted to run away. I could not walk normally, my legs hurt, and I was hobbling. As I was walking, I remembered the warmth and safety with which Bob's parents had always welcomed me, so I made up my mind to take refuge with my friend Bob and his parents.

With every step, I was becoming more and more determined not to return home. It was a little boy's sincere desire. But not all desires can come true. Bob was already awake from his nap when I appeared at the door. There was a look of concern on their faces when Bob and his parents saw me beaten and hobbling. Bob's mother pulled up my T-shirt, and when she saw all those bruises, she got quite a shock. She led me to the bathroom, took off my clothes, and gently washed my body. Then she brought me some of Bob's clothes to put on. She saw how scared I was and let me sleep over. Meanwhile, my mother got back home and realized that I was not there. She got worried, thinking something bad might have happened to me. She looked for me everywhere in the neighborhood, and in the end, she knocked on Bob's door. I felt sorry for my mother, who was crying, and that made tears come to my eyes too. For a moment, I forgot about the pain. The two mothers talked for quite a while, and I heard when my mother thanked Bob's mother for her help. They agreed that it would be best for me to stay there for the night. The fear stayed with me the next morning. After breakfast, Bob's mother held me in her arms and tried to comfort me. She could feel I was scared and upset. I did not want to go home because I was scared of my father and getting beaten again. But my mother showed up, and I had to leave. On our way home, I was in pain, trembling with fear while my mother was trying to comfort me, saying that my father was not at home and that I had no reason to worry. Her words calmed me down a little bit. She held my hand tightly and made me feel safe.

Sometimes in life, we are pushed beyond our limits. In my early years, I lived my life in constant fear and struggle. I endured abuse, sleepless nights, hardships, and beatings. I do not know how I survived, but I prayed to God as my mother taught me. In spite of all sufferings, I always managed to think positively, although there were not many happy moments in my childhood. Life has taught me that success is not only to be happy when you have everything but also to find your inner strength and keep your chin up when you do not have anything. It is easy to play in the sun, but you must learn to play in the rain as well. A lot of things kept coming to my mind on my way home. I dreamed of a better life in which my father did not drink and was good to me. I dreamed that my family lived in harmony, that there was enough food for all of us. I also dreamed of the juices I saw other children drink. Most of all, I wished my father was different. All I could do was dream, but I could not change reality. My mother and I came back home, and the fear of my father overcame me again. My father was not at home, and at least I was happy for a moment. My house seemed to me like the house of terror I once saw at the local fair. It was filled with fear and devoid of beautiful memories.

On another occasion, I was playing with some kids on the playground when my drunken father appeared. For no reason, he grabbed my ankle and lifted me up in the air. Then he hit my back on the electric pole. At that moment, my mouth opened, but I could not breathe. I saw the bright sun turning into total darkness, and I thought that I would die. After a short time, I started to breathe again. Thank God my father did not hit me on the head. I surely would have died there. A neighbor saw all this and screamed at my father. Then my father ran away as usual. My neighbor brought me home. My mom was shocked when she heard what had happened to me. She put me to bed and tried to comfort me. I had such pain in my back that I could not get out of bed for a couple of months. At this point, my father stopped drinking for a while because he was scared that I would not recover.

My father was a house painter. He worked to supplement his low pension. The house owners gave him alcohol to drink, so our problems continued. He did not see they were taking advantage of him. His work was paid in brandy. We were all afraid of him when he was drunk. One night, he came home drunk again. I heard his voice. I heard him singing. It gave me a chill to the bone. At that moment, I wanted to be swallowed up by the earth or simply disappear. I could not withstand the agony, his beatings, the crying, and the running away from him and from myself. I tried to stay calm and act normally, but at the same time, I was ready to die. I thought to myself, *If my father wants to kill me, let it be*, as life itself was not any better than death. I heard my father's footsteps at the door. Fear gripped me. He opened the door and stepped into the room. I stood still, with my eyes wide open, waiting for what might happen. My father looked straight at me with his piercing eyes. It was too late to hide under the bed, so I decided to get out of his way. My mother came closer to me to protect me. It encouraged me. I noticed that she was afraid of my father too. She was shaking like a leaf in the wind. My father did not care about that. He asked for something to eat. My mother went to serve him dinner. He took the opportunity and hit me. I fell down. I did not have time to think about the pain. I tried to get away, thinking I might get another blow. My father turned to hit me again, but my mother jumped in. She pushed him away from me, yelling at him. He did not care about her yelling, and he shook his head and started eating. When he finished, he came up with a new idea to punish me.

He told me I was to sit awake on the chair next to his bed while he was sleeping. He threatened to beat me if I fell asleep. My mother could not do anything about it because she was scared of my father too. It was hard for me to be close to my father and even harder for a young boy not to fall asleep when everyone else was sleeping. So all night long, I was sitting on the chair trying to stay awake. Time passed, and it was getting harder and harder for me to resist the urge to sleep. The light in the room was on, but it did not help me either. I got very tired, my eyelids started to droop, my head tilted to one side, and at some point, I fell asleep. During the night, my father woke up, probably to go to the bathroom. He saw me sleeping on the chair, so he slapped me so hard that I fell on the floor. I did not know where I was. "Why are you sleeping?" he asked angrily. I did not know what to say. What could I have said after such a blow? I chose to remain silent and leave it all to fate. My mother got up and held me in her arms. Such was my childhood—one loving parent, the other abusive. My mother stayed awake all night. The next morning, my father apologized to me about the night before. His insincere apology did not matter to me. *The right actions in the future are the best apologies for bad actions in the past*, I thought. You have to show that you are taking responsibility for the things you have said and done. Neither breakfast nor my father's apology mattered to me that morning. I couldn't wait to run out of the house so as not to be around my father.

All I wanted was to forget what happened the night before. Hanging out with Bob was my refuge from painful memories. Bob usually got up at about nine o'clock. I waited for him impatiently at his garden gate to come out so that the two of us could play. I waited and waited but couldn't make the time pass faster. Bob's mother noticed me and invited me inside the house. Bob was still sleeping. Bob's mother had a plan for us to have breakfast together. She explained to me that Bob had a better appetite when we ate together. I was glad to have a tasty breakfast. We had a lot of fun playing together. We even invented our own games, and we often made toys from stuff we found around. In the middle of the game, Bob's mom called both of us for lunch. I felt ashamed but at the same time, glad to have lunch with them. They were a wonderful and dear family that gave me a lot of love and comfort. After lunch, Bob went to take his afternoon nap as usual, and I just wandered around, trying to avoid going home. There were a lot of other children in the neighborhood, and I played with some of them. That dark afternoon clouds filled the sky and soon brought rain. We had to stop playing and run home.

My brother Rick, as a child, willfully went astray. With his friend, he used to steal and beg for money on the streets, and he rarely came home. Our bad family situation drove him to crime. When I was six, Rick wanted to get me into his dirty business. I was a little boy and, in his opinion, thus ideal for stealing. My neighbor Seth, Marijan's peer, saved me from being led astray. He knew what my brother's intention was, so he grabbed my arm and dragged me away from the bad company. I thought that anything else, even crime, would have been better than living with an alcoholic father. Seth taught me that crime was not the way out. I am grateful to him for that life lesson. My brother Marijan, even as a child, was very selfish. He only thought about himself and his needs. He never shared food with the rest of the family. He spent a lot of time at the neighbors' and with his buddies. He mainly came home when my father was not drunk or was in a good mood. Nance was like Marijan. She also spent a lot of time in the neighborhood. Although she had meals there, she would come home and eat with us. Food was often the main reason for disagreements. Gina and I always got the worst. We even got beaten by our brother and sister if we asked for some more food. We could not understand why Nance and Marijan were so selfish.

I was hoping that frequent injustice would cease over time. I was also hoping that the beatings and poverty would end when I grew up. That was the reason why I wanted to grow up as quickly as possible. Later in life, I learned that everything is transient, but then I was young at the very beginning of my life, and my fortune cookie was yet to be earned. I thought about all this until late every evening. And again, I went to bed on an empty stomach. My father did not come home that night. He stayed in a bar. Since he was away, the house was so peaceful, and I could at least be a little happy that night. As a gift from heaven, a surprise awaited us in the morning. Our neighbor Doris called my mother and gave her half a pot of stew. As my mother brought it into the house, my stomach fluttered with joy. We could not afford the luxury of choosing whether to have bacon and eggs or stew for breakfast. We ate anything just to feel our stomach full. My mother quickly warmed up the stew, and we ate it with relish. Our dear neighbor Doris gave us a feast every time she brought leftovers from her home. She was a good cook, and her meals were the best gifts in the world. We often did not have enough money to buy groceries because my father chose to spend all the money he earned on alcohol only, and my mother, who did the laundry for people, did not work every day.

One afternoon, my father came home drunk and brought along a whore with him. He threw all of us out of the house. My mother started weeping and wailing, trying to prevent them from entering our home, but in vain. Although drunk, my father was physically stronger than she was. He just pushed my mother out of his way and got into the house with the whore. All that noise attracted the neighbors' attention and made them curious. There were a lot of boozers in our area, but even to them, bringing a whore to their own home, in front of their wives and children, was an utterly incomprehensible act. Some women from the neighborhood tried to comfort my mother and advised her to leave her husband. They wondered whether it was reasonable to live with such an immoral husband in a bad marriage. My mom's heart was breaking. She knew that she was stuck in a bad marriage, that she was with a man rotten to the core, but she was afraid to go on with her life alone with five children. However, that night, she found the courage to leave her husband. After having sex with the whore, my father fell asleep. Marijan and Nance were somewhere in the neighborhood that night, Rick was with his buddies, and only Gina and I were at home. My mother took us, and we embarked on embracing uncertainty.

Darkness had already fallen. My mother's plan was to spend the night at our friends' who lived on the other side of the city. We did not know if they would take us in, but we had to try because my mother had no intention of turning back. It was pitch dark as we walked down the street full of pot-holes. We were afraid that drivers coming from the opposite direction might not notice us while we were blinded by the headlights of their cars. My mother held our hands tightly as we were walking. Our fear was somewhat eased by our brave mother's soothing words and tight grip. I believe she was scared as well. There were no streetlights, and we barely managed to avoid getting hit by the cars. Some dogs came out of nowhere, barking at us. My mother tried to protect us. Then we got an idea to use some rocks. I filled my pockets with them and firmly squeezed one in my hand. We defended ourselves by throwing rocks at the dogs. This kept them at a reasonable distance from us. We walked several miles barefoot and got cuts and bruises on our dusty feet, but we did not give up. I am sure that in hard times like this one, God alone saved us and helped us get through.

We were slowly approaching our destination. Our friends lived in a city quarter called Senjak. It was a suburban area a few miles from our house. There was less traffic, the streets were wider, and there were streetlights, so we felt safer. Our friends had six children and lived in a small house. We did not worry about the lack of space in their house. We were ready to sleep on the floor. We worried because this friend of ours had a drinking problem too, and we did not know if he was in a good mood. We arrived at the door of their house. It was the point of no return. My mother hesitated for a moment then gently knocked on the door waiting in great anticipation for someone to answer. We were exhausted from everything that had happened to us that day, and we believed that our salvation would come in the end.

Lisa opened the door. She was surprised but at the same time, aware why we had come. She knew all about our problems. Her husband also drank a lot, but he did not behave as badly as my father did. She invited us in. Tired and covered in dust, we must have looked like street bums. There was a water tap in their yard, so we washed ourselves a little. I also emptied my pockets and threw away the rocks. I was free from anxiety. It felt like the burden I had been carrying just fell off my shoulders. Gina and Mother felt carefree too. The hosts placed some mattresses on the floor for us to sleep. They were stuffed with dried corn husks. As we lay, a big cloud of dust rose from the mattresses, but it did not bother us. We were tired but happy that we had a roof over our heads. We just wanted to have a good night's sleep. Gina and I fell asleep immediately, whereas my mother stayed awake for a while talking with our hosts.

The night was short, or it just seemed to have gone by fast. We had to get up at the crack of dawn. As I have already said, our friends lived in a cramped house, and their children, who were getting ready for school, could not move around because of the mattresses we had slept on. Great apprehension troubled us that morning. Our kind hosts served us breakfast, but we could not expect anything else as they were in a difficult situation too. So how could they help us? We had no idea what to do or where to go. That question taunted us during breakfast.

As soon as we finished our breakfast, someone knocked on the door. It was my father. How did he know that we were here? That was my first thought. The moment he walked through the door, he started begging my mother to come back home, apologizing for everything he had done. We had heard those apologies so many times before. As I saw him at the door, my bad feelings for him reappeared. I was petrified of him, and I did not have any love for him in my heart. I could not even stand being in his presence. I despised him for what he had been doing to my mother. My mother was having second thoughts. On the one hand, she did not know where to go with us, all five children. On the other hand, my father's words did not sound convincing to her. My father started promising her the stars and the moon. He promised that he would change his behavior, stop drinking, and treat his family better. His words did not carry much weight. It was alcohol doing the talking all too often, not him. That was why the whole family was suffering. Over the years of a bad marriage, my mother had become truly dissatisfied, drained, and vulnerable. Yet she decided to go back home. She was aware of his lies, his unnecessary roughness, and his failed, unrealistic expectations and promises, but financial dependence on my father and the inferior status of women in society at that time made her change her mind. She hoped he would change eventually.

We said goodbye to our friends, and my father took us home. It was very painful for me. It was even harder than the night before when we had been trying to find our way through the dark, being chased by the dogs and scared of the cars. With every step, I was becoming more and more resentful. I did not want to go home, and I felt like the Almighty was pulling me back as far as possible from the pain and suffering. My father went on with his promises all the way home. He kept saying that he would be a better husband, a better father, and that he would not drink anymore. *He would drink neither more nor less than he already had*, I thought ironically. It was a double play on words. I did not want to listen to my father's empty words. I had heard them too many times before. All our neighbors were surprised to see us back home. They were shocked that my mother had forgiven my father for his actions. Unfortunately, we did not have a better option, so we had to return home. That day, my father played the role of a good husband. He decided to cook beans for lunch. He was a good cook, but he cooked only on rare occasions. My mother was delighted with his gesture. It seemed that my father did this deliberately, knowing what could make my mother happy. Anyway, the lunch was delicious.

The tasty meal and a bit of peace in our home repressed the previous day's memories. Too many bad memories were stuck in my little head, so I wanted to make room for a little joy.

We lived in a working-class neighborhood, composed primarily of single-family homes and small apartment buildings. Both the middle class and poor families with lots of children lived here. We all knew each other very well and generally relied on one another. In the case of a big celebration or great misfortune, the neighbors were the first to help. People hung out together, drinking coffee or chatting endlessly. Although there were some family feuds and gossiping among them, it was a decent neighborhood to live in.

Our first neighbors were Mister Stan and his wife Nancy. They had two sons. Nancy liked to drink, and we could often see her drunk. Mr. Stan would sometimes drink a lot of alcohol but not too often. He was protective toward his sons, and they did not suffer because of their mother's drinking problem. Bob and Ann lived next door to them. They had no children of their own, so they adopted a boy named John. John was about eleven or twelve years older than me. He was a nice boy. Unfortunately, his parents, Bob and Ann, were alcoholics, but they were not abusive. Not far from them lived Peter and Jen, the couple with lots of children. Peter drank excessively, perhaps even more than my father. It was difficult to say who was worse. They were both alcoholics with a bad temper. There was also a Romani family in our neighborhood. Michael was an alcoholic, and his wife, as I remember, was a kind and nice woman. Another alcoholic, George, lived next door to them. He also had a big family. If we had had a club in our neighborhood, it would have been named "The Club of Alcoholics." What a destructive and depressed neighborhood it was!

My father and our first neighbors, Stan and Nancy, used to be good friends, but then they had a fight. We did not know the reason for their fight, but we assumed it had something to do with alcohol. One day, we heard the distressing news that Nancy had passed away. I think the year was 1966. Stan was crushed. Their two sons were older than me but far from being able to take care of themselves. Back then, it was a custom to keep the deceased in the house for a day or two before the funeral and to organize the procession from the house to the cemetery. Relatives, friends, neighbors, and acquaintances would come to the house of the deceased to express their condolences to the family. For the local lowlifes, it was an opportunity to get some food and, what was more important for them, some alcohol.

Anyway, all the neighbors gathered to help Stan organize the funeral. My parents helped too. Tragedies like this one were the opportunity to forget about disagreements and to offer a helping hand. After the funeral, almost everybody came back to Stan's house for the reception. It was also one of the customs. The lunch was served to commemorate the deceased. Relatives and friends evoked the memories of the deceased and sympathized with the family members.

The night after Nancy's funeral, Gina and I played at home. As we did not have a TV, our games were the only way to pass the time and have fun. My father did not drink much that day. He felt sorry about our neighbor's death, so he left us alone. Gina and I played till late that night. Suddenly, at around midnight, we heard some strange sounds coming from somewhere outside. Soon, one of them stood out. No doubt, it was the voice of our neighbor Nancy. We were absolutely sure about that. The eerie voice seemed to be coming in through one of our windows, and we could clearly hear Nancy calling out my father's name. A chill ran down my spine. Actually, we all stood still dazed, struck with horror. We had put some nylon on the window that father had broken before in one of his drunken moments. Now the nylon fluttered strangely, and suddenly, the outline of Nancy's face appeared, calling my father to come out. With a light-brown complexion, messy hair, bloody eyes and teeth, she was staring at us. I was so frightened that I started crying. My father took me on his lap. He was scared too. For the first time in my life, he hugged me. That did not calm me down either. I could still see Nancy's face in our window, and I kept crying. My mother came closer to me, trying to calm me down, but in vain. My heart was beating fast as if it were going to jump out of my chest. We were all paralyzed with fear. My father brought an old hammer, put it into my hand, and together, we started hitting the floor repeatedly. We hoped the noise would chase the ghost away. But it did not help. The situation became even worse. We heard some strange noise coming from the dresser, and the drawers were opening and closing. Then we heard a voice coming first from one side of the room and then from the other. It was the voice of our dead neighbor. She was still staring at us from the broken window. Maddened by fear, we thought we would not survive the night. Dread-filled we were waiting for the dawn.

As the night was passing, the eerie voice was fading away. We all breathed a sigh of relief. It was the scariest night of my life. The morning finally came. We were tired, afraid, and confused. The neighbors came to visit us. Perhaps they had heard something during the night. My parents told them what had happened in our home. They were stunned. Gina fearlessly took the piece of nylon from the window on which there was still the brownish face of the dead neighbor. Gina tried to wash it off, but it stayed there. My father then took that piece of nylon and gave it to Stan, showing him the demonic face of his wife. Stan looked at us in disbelief. We did not understand what Nancy wanted from us or what she wanted to say to our father. We wondered why her soul did not rest in peace and if she would come back again. My brother told me that she did come back several times after this incident, but I don't remember that. This was already scary enough for me. The mystery remained unsolved. Only occasionally did we speak about it in a whisper.

Being alone after his wife's death was very difficult for Stan, especially with two children to take care of. He was trying to drown his sorrows in alcohol. My father did not want to leave Stan alone, so they drank together. A few neighbors accompanied them. Very soon, they drank up all the brandy they could find at Stan's. That did not stop them. They had no boundaries when it came to drinking. They went to Timothy when they ran out.

Timothy and his wife lived in our neighborhood too. They were a wealthy middle-aged couple. They had a big yard. Tim and his wife lived in a separate house, and their sons lived with their families in their own houses in the same yard. Timothy earned a living from selling pickled vegetables, tomato sauce, sour cabbage, and similar products. He also made and sold poor quality brandy. His customers were mostly poor people, so he often sold them very bad quality alcohol. Tim was a strict man, and he always managed to get money for his goods. When the "drinking buddies" drank up all the brandy at Stan's, they headed to Tim's for some more. Tim received them with open arms, glad to have somebody to sell his brandy to. He set the chairs for them in the backyard and brought as much brandy as they could drink. They drank and drank until they passed out. They stumbled and fumbled, trying to help each other, but in vain. In the end, they fell to the ground, wallowing like pigs in the mud until some of their family members came to take them home.

Our mother carried and dragged our father all the way home. My mother was thin and tiny, so even today, I have no idea how she found the strength to do that. My drunken father fell and rolled on the ground. He asked my mother for dinner, and she served it to him. He took a few bites, mumbling that the dinner was not tasty, and threw the plate on the ground. He must have been too drunk to know what it tasted like. Then it got even worse. He angrily grabbed the pot with food and threw it on the ground as well. This was supposed to be our lunch for the next day, but now it was on the ground. Since we had no money to buy more groceries, my mother could not cook another meal. My father spent the rest of the night in pain, sobbing, whining, and calling for help. He complained that all his muscles and bones hurt. He asked our mother for a massage to relieve the pain. Lying in agony, he swore that he would never drink again. I did not have peace and quiet that night, but at least I was sure that my father would not beat me. The next day, my father was still feeling sick but not as sick as the previous night. Thus, he spent the whole day in the house. The next day he got better, and as soon as he recovered, he rushed to find some brandy to make up for the lost time.

He did not go far looking for brandy. He went over to our neighbor Wally, who gave him some to drink. All of a sudden, Wally got a crazy idea for fun. He told my father that he would give him more brandy to drink if my father pulled out his tooth. My father grabbed a piece of rusty barbed wire from Wally's fence and stuck it into his mouth. Since he was drunk, he did not feel the pain. He pulled out several teeth, damaging the others, and cut his lips and mouth. It seemed that he would bleed out, so they urgently took him to the hospital. The doctors had to pull out the rest of his teeth due to the level of his injuries, and they kept him in the hospital for medical treatment. My father spent some time in the hospital, and maybe it's not nice to say, but we enjoyed that period. There was no yelling and harassing in the house.

Even after leaving the hospital, my father felt ill. He had had all his teeth pulled out, so he had difficulty chewing and swallowing food. He could not eat solid food, so my mother had to prepare him soft food. The doctors prescribed him some medicine and strictly forbade him to drink alcohol. As drinking alcohol while taking medicine could be fatal, my father stopped drinking. It was such a relief to all of us. Nance and Marijan came back home. It was a heavenly period. Only Rick carried on in the same way as before. He continued with petty thefts and begging with his mates. He visited us from time to time. The period of my father's abstinence from alcohol, I remember as a happy one. I changed too. I spent more time at home. My father was preoccupied with his health problems and pain, so he paid no attention to us. Instead of running away, we now stayed at home playing together, and I stopped being afraid of my father.

We were poor, we had almost nothing, and we were humble. We appreciated the little things, and we lived, as I have already mentioned, in a shabby little room with no furniture. There was a small old chest of drawers in which we kept everything. There were my parents' bed and a bunk bed in which we, the children, slept. Depending on how many children were at home, we would make combinations of how many of us would sleep in that bed. To complete the list, I have to mention the old rusty stove. During cold winter days, we were happy to have it to warm us up. Winters in Serbia can be very cold.

Our house was by the side of a macadam road, which the workers walked along when going to or coming back from work. Further down the road were the fields where people planted gardens and grew corn or crops. It happened one night at the end of the summer around 10:45 p.m., the time when the second shift workers returned home from the factories. We did not usually hear them. Exhausted after a hard day's work, they would walk home in silence or quietly speaking. But that night, we heard shouts. Somebody was shouting, "Fire, fire! Help!" My father went out, and we ran after him. A big fire had caught a cornfield. It was Tim's cornfield. Many people stood at a safe distance from the fire. Some of them were waving, pointing at something in the field. We ran toward the fire and found an unbelievable sight before our eyes. What prevented the people from putting out the fire was a large candle which could clearly be seen floating just above the ground, moving left and right continuously, spreading its flame throughout the cornfield. "It's the devil's work," somebody said. Even Tim, the owner of the field, was looking at the demonic candle astonished, not having the courage to put out the fire. The fire desolated the field quickly. Then it stopped and did not spread any further. The people started to scatter, but nobody had the courage to pass by the burnt field. They took some different pathways home.

At dawn the next morning, Tim rushed with his family to check what was left after the fire. Still in fear and convinced that the fire was an act of the devil himself or some other paranormal force, they paced carefully, fearing they might step on some magical trap that could put a bigger curse on them. Rummaging through the ashes, they found a dead turtle on whose shell there was still a piece of candle stuck with wax. So the mysterious case of arson was solved. Someone put a burning candle on the top of the turtle and let it roam around the field. There were neither demons nor paranormal forces. Who had really done it remained a mystery forever. Whether it had been a bad joke or the revenge of a dissatisfied customer on Tim for his poor quality brandy was never revealed. The story of the burnt cornfield was retold over and over again for many years to come, and every now and then, someone would shake their head at hearing about the turtle and the candle.

As I am telling you these stories, they remind me of so many other things. Not far from our house stood a big old shack which was used as a bus stop. People used it to take shelter from bad weather while waiting for their bus. The shack could fit a lot of people. The biggest crowds came when workers left for work. There could be coming four or five buses at that time. All children from the neighborhood liked to play in that shack. One afternoon, the workers were waiting, as usual, to take their buses to the factories. The protagonists in this story were Jason and Brad. They were next-door neighbors, and they both worked at the same factory. Brad had had his eye removed. As a matter of fact, he had a glass eye. The buses arrived. As usual, people started pushing each other to board the bus as quickly as they could. Those buses were equipped with a small number of seats, so most of the people had to stand while traveling. As expected, everybody wanted to get on the bus first and take a seat. Somehow in this tumult of confusion, Jason stumbled and fell in front of the bus door. Nobody even noticed that, or at least Brad didn't. Trying to fight for the best position to board the bus, he focused on the bus without noticing that he stepped on Jason, who was lying on the ground. To make things worse, he stepped on his neck. Poor Jason was trying to crawl out of the tight position, pushing Brad's foot off his neck. At some point, Brad felt something grab his ankle, so he looked down. Surprised, he saw Jason lying and fighting for breath. "What are you doing down there?" he asked Jason. Whether Jason turned red due to a lack of air to breathe or because he was mad at reckless Brad was unknown. As they were good friends and good neighbors, they made up quickly, and the incident remained an anecdote which was always retold with a smile.

As father was sober for a few months, the period of peace and tranquility continued. We still did not have enough money, but I remember these days as quality time in my life. I remember being almost seven years old when my parents informed us that my mother was pregnant. With all the confusion and horror in my life, I did not know that it meant we were going to have a baby in the house. My father somehow became better and more sensitive. The pregnancy seemed to have a positive impact on him. It was February 22, 1967. Only Gina and I were at home when my mother started feeling strong and intense pain. She started crying, and then the two of us started crying because our mother was suffering. She sent us for our neighbor Jen. Jen came quickly. Gina and I stayed outside, waiting to see what was going to happen. And soon, our baby sister was born at candlelight (there was no electricity in the shack). Our parents named her Snezana. We were all happy, whereas my father was a bit concerned. He was probably thinking about how to raise a baby with so little money in a cramped house.

The next day, a lot of neighbors and friends came over to congratulate our parents. Almost everybody brought presents for the baby, mostly money and clothes. A lot of diapers and good quality food were needed for Mother and the baby, but we did not know how to provide all that. My father's enthusiasm for the baby did not last long. With each passing day, he was becoming more and more aware of the situation he had gotten into, and as many times before, when he was in trouble, he reached for alcohol. Our mother alone took care of the baby, and she did it with lots of love and an unbelievable willingness to do her best. Despite her tiny figure, she was like a lioness to me, with the strength of cosmic magnitude, bold, protective, fearless, and selfless when it came to taking care of her children.

The winter of 1967 was rather long. At the beginning of March, it was still very cold with plenty of snow, and we ran out of firewood. We did not have money to buy some more. Luckily, a firewood seller felt pity for us and sold us some firewood on credit. Furthermore, he delivered us the firewood. A cubic meter of logs was unloaded outside the shack. It was up to us to cut and bring them in. My mother was busy handling the baby, Marijan and Nance were at school, so Gina and I helped our father out. First, we put those big logs in a pile next to the shack, and then my father himself cut and chopped them. Gina and I were too young to use a handsaw or an ax, but we tried hard to carry the chopped firewood inside. It was really hard and tiring work, and my feet were freezing cold. I could feel the wet snow through the holes in my torn shoes, but I did not mind. I thought how all of us, including my little sister Snezana, would soon be enjoying ourselves by a cozy log fire in our home. I have to admit that I enjoyed watching our father work not only because it was nice to see him work for the benefit of the family for a change but also because the work kept him busy, so he did not have time to think about alcohol and drinking.

Marijan and Nance were already in higher grades of primary school. Nance was in sixth grade, and Marijan was in eighth grade. He was a bad student. He hung out with other unruly and difficult students. They seemed to be competing to see who would get more *F*s. The end of the school year was near. A week before the end, Marijan had eight *F*s. Improving so many bad grades in such a short time would be a challenge for the best students, even Einstein himself, let alone for Marijan. The day of the parent-teacher meeting arrived. My mother could not leave the baby alone, so my father went to the meeting. He was drunk as usual. He patiently listened to the teacher who handed out the report cards and informed the parents about the performance and behavior of their children. He waited for all the parents to leave. Then he approached the teacher, grabbed her blouse, pulled her long chin left, and right, and then asked her, "Why didn't my son pass?" The scared woman tried to explain that Marijan neither had been studying nor trying enough in school. My father grabbed her by the neck and started pulling her again. The terrified woman began screaming at him to let her go, but he did not loosen his grip.

Crying and sobbing, she kept repeating, "Everything will be all right. Everything will be okay." My father let her go. And everything was all right. Miraculously, all of Marijan's grades were improved, and he passed the year and finished primary school. For some reason, my father was not reported to the police. I guess the teacher had had enough of both problematic Marijan and our father and that she did not want to see them ever again.

It was the era of epic heroes in the movies and books. Children identified with them and imitated them. The Roman legions, ancient Egyptians, Gauls wearing mustaches went from the film screens into the children's games around the neighborhood in no time. My brother Marijan's favorite hero was Prince Valiant. I don't know where Marijan had seen that film, but the next day, he begged our father to make him a suitable costume. My father was very skillful. From wood, some old tin, and who knows what else, he made a shield, helmet, and a sword, which looked really nice. The sword had a wonderful scabbard. He also made a trumpet. Marijan was thrilled, and so were the other children from the neighborhood when they saw him. They were so delighted that almost everyone came to our father, begging him to make something similar for them. Of course, our father did not refuse.

Soon, the whole army of medieval knights was marching through our neighborhood. I don't know whether the knights in the Middle Ages were so noisy, but these were. The whole neighborhood was echoing with the sounds of their fights and games. I was too young to play with them, but I enjoyed watching them. Masked and engaged in their game, they looked like an acting troupe or some sort of film crew performing right in front of me. The game became very popular. The boys from the other streets saw our boys, and soon the fathers throughout the town had to make the whole arsenal of wooden swords and shields and similar things. After the armies in the neighborhood were formed and armed, the first confrontation started. Children from one neighborhood would war against their peers from the other one. That was how our boys arranged the fight with the boys from the nearby area. Our knights took the upcoming fights very seriously. The beginning of the war was scheduled a few days later. To prepare the best they could, they asked our father, an experienced WW II soldier, for help. He gave them some useful advice, and a very deep and long defense trench was dug out soon. They even dug out a hole, almost six feet deep, to hold future prisoners of war.

The day of the crucial battle arrived. About fifteen boys heavily armed with wooden swords led by Marijan embarked on a conquest of the neighboring area. When the trumpet sounded, the battle started. The movement of our troops was soon spotted by the children from the neighboring area. They organized themselves, buckled up their swords, and the two armies went to meet each other. It was a true masquerade that I observed from a safe distance. The battle took place in a small field where we occasionally played. Standing opposite each other, they first mocked each other then provoked each other and bragged. Soon afterward, they rushed at one another, and the clash of two armies was violent and terrifying. It seemed as if the swords were made of some solid and thick wood as loud clanging could be heard. They were hitting each other very hard. You could hear screams while the battle was raging. There were some funny but efficient solutions in the war arsenal. Mike, one of our soldiers, tied a rope around an old aluminum jug and used it as a mace. He swung with his jug and hit the opponents, some in the leg, some in the arm, and some even in the head. The battle lasted for a long time, perhaps an hour or so. Because of their ignorance, it seemed more like a club fight than the knights' battle. There were many torn shirts, bruises, and even some bleeding wounds. Little by little, Marijan's army pushed away the opponents. At first, they backed away slowly, and then, having realized that they were tired and overpowered, they decided to retreat from the battlefield. It was a complete triumph for Marijan's army. They won a few war trophies and captured two prisoners. They gloriously took them to our camp. The victory celebration had just started when the leaders of the defeated army came to us, waving the white flag. They came to admit the defeat and to retrieve the two prisoners because their parents were impatiently waiting for them at home for lunch. The boys from the two confronted clans shook hands and made up. They were good friends again as they had been before this "Prince Valiant" battle.

Reflecting on my childhood, I cannot leave out the story about our neighbor Bob and his wife Sabrina. Sabrina was a good but uneducated woman. It was not unusual for women to be uneducated in Yugoslavia before WW II. Her husband, Bob, finished a few years of primary school until Hitler threw him and all students out of school. This is my metaphorical thinking about Bob because all school was ended in small villages like ours after the start of World War II. Afterward, even though he was only about thirteen years old, he worked and supported his family. They did not have children. There was a story about Sabrina, which followed her throughout her entire life. The alleged event took place in the same neighborhood several years after WW II. Sabrina ran out of money for groceries, so she went to her neighbor to borrow a few dinars. To be more specific, she asked for five dinars. She intended to pay her back in a few days from Bob's next salary. The neighbor did not have five dinars in change, only a ten-dinar note, so she told Sabrina, "I only have ten dinars, I don't have five."

Allegedly, Sabrina replied sadly, "All right, if you don't have five, at least give me those ten dinars." That was how the story, which spread around the neighborhood, described nice Sabrina as someone who did not know that ten dinars are more than five. Unlike her, Bob was good with money, maybe even too good.

Somewhere in the 1960s, it was recorded that there was a vampire in Smederevo. Speaking of vampires, the word vampire is the only word of Serbian origin that has made it onto the international stage. The vampire from Smederevo had a regular appearance pattern. The road from the isolated facilities of the steel plant in Smederevo was passing by the old cemetery. That was exactly where the vampire awaited and intercepted his victims. His victims were mostly women who were going back home alone from work late at night. The vampire would jump out from behind a tombstone or a bush and scare the women with his macabre appearance. The victims would, in fear, throw away everything they were carrying, including their bags and purses, and run away as far and fast as they could. Vampire attacks were more frequent on payday. One night, a few women were returning home from work together. That day, they got their monthly salary. When they approached the cemetery, the vampire rushed at them, growling. Terrified, the women threw their handbags and ran away, screaming. Pale and voiceless, they ran into a nearby pub. The owner tried to help them recover from the shock by giving them some cold water and sugar. When they pulled themselves together a little bit, the women explained what had happened to them.

There was a big guy sitting at the bar, a truck driver by profession, whom no one knew by name, but simply called him Bosanac after his mother-land Bosnia. He was listening carefully to the whole story. He drank up the brandy he was sipping, took another shot bottoms up, and then stood up from the bar. Determined to solve the mystery, Bosanac headed to the cemetery. Realizing that a big guy was approaching him and having no place to hide, the vampire jumped in front of him, screaming and hissing at him. Bosanac apparently was not a person who believed in stories about vampires. He grabbed the vampire and started beating him. After a few blows, the vampire started crying out, "Stop! Please don't hurt me! I'm not a vampire!" The vampire took off the rags and the sheet he was wrapped in, and our neighbor Bob appeared before Bosanac. The police arrived soon and confiscated the money Bob had taken from the women. The money was returned to the victims, and Bob was sent to prison for a while. He justified himself by not having a job and thus being made to attack and rob people. That was how Bosanac, to whom the poor women were endlessly grateful, solved the mystery of Smederevo's vampire. The time spent in prison had a positive influence on Bob. He changed a lot, improved himself, and after he got out of prison, he started a fair and orderly life.

Many years later, one summer night, an idle neighbor Wally and a couple of young men recalled the story of Bob the Vampire and decided to play a joke on him. They gathered under Bob's window. If we are to believe their side of the story, it happened like this. Peeking through the torn curtains on the window, Wally and the other young men saw Sabrina helping Bob bathe. The young men started making inarticulate sounds and banging on the window. Sabrina got scared and muttered through clenched teeth, "My heart, my heart!" Bob was allegedly drunk, and at first, he did not realize that by "my heart, my heart," Sabrina was not sweet-talking to him. Her heart was pounding with fear. When he pulled himself together and realized what was happening, he grabbed an ax and rushed out. In the meantime, Wally and his friends hid on the woodshed roof. Being overwrought, Bob looked for the bastards around the yard. According to Wally, he found a piece of brick on the roof and threw it at Bob. He did not hit him, but he scared him to death because Bob immediately ran into the house and locked the door. Luckily, the consequences of the incident were not that terrible. Sabrina's blood pressure went up, but soon, she calmed down. The next day, the incident was retold around the neighborhood. Some laughed, some shook their heads in disapproval of Wally's joke, and others wondered whether the story was made up. However, Bob became known as Bob the Vampire from that day on.

Days, months, years passed by, the seasons changed, everything changed, only our poverty remained. We mostly lived on what other people would give us. Good people gave us their old clothes or shoes, but we were over the moon every time we got food. Our neighbors and friends would some-times give us their lunch leftovers. Those were holi-day meals for us.

In the summer of 1967, I was told to prepare myself for starting school. It is a big milestone in every child's life. I was proud of myself. I felt like a grown-up, and it was bringing me joy. What made me even happier was the fact that my friend Bob was also starting school. We were both hoping that we would be in the same class. In August, future first graders were supposed to go to the school psycholo-gist for preschool testing and an assessment of their readiness for school. My mother took me to the test-ing, and Bob's mother took him too. There were lots of children there. The test itself was not particularly difficult—a few basic questions about our family members, such as how many brothers or sisters we had, our parents' names, and where we lived. Then there were some simple math questions and some about geometric shapes. I passed the test. All the way home, I was skipping joyfully, but my mother was worried. I was looking forward to starting school while my mother was worried about getting all the necessary school supplies for me.

Being all excited, I went to see Bob straight away. We talked about our impressions of the testing. It was obvious that he was happy to start school soon. We believed that starting school meant we were not little kids anymore and that we were about to start an exciting new chapter in our lives. If only we could be in the same class. As we were talking about school and what was waiting for us there, Bob and I got to a beautiful flower field by the road. We used to come here very often to observe bees. We were fascinated by these hardworking, determined little creatures. There were so many of them. They were busy flying from flower to flower, sipping nectar. Then they would mysteriously fly away, but the new ones would always come performing their waggle dances in circles like it was some kind of a rule only known to them.

Bob tried to catch a bee. We knew how to do it. We would catch them and, with a light but firm touch, hold all their fragile wings together, being careful not to squeeze them and thus get stung. This time, Bob made a mistake. He did not hold the bee properly. It wriggled out of his hand and stung him. "Ouch!" he yelled in pain! A red bump developed around the sting. He started flapping his hand, then rubbing the painful spot. I think he even cried. It obviously hurt him a lot. I felt sorry for Bob. As a good friend, he always shared his toys with me, but now he wanted to share his angry bee experience with me. He tried to talk me into provoking a bee to sting me. *Hmm, why not? I'll give it a try*, I thought. Never before had I been stung by a bee. As this would probably cheer up my friend whose eyes were still glistening with tears and his cheeks wet, I bent down and put my hand over the flowers while the bees were buzzing around. Bob gave me instructions. I grabbed a bee by the wings as he told me. The bee wriggled out and jabbed its barbed stinger into my hand. "Ouch, ouch!" Now I started to cry. It was very uncomfortable. I felt burning pain and itching in my hand. While Bob was giggling, I was jumping up and down, screaming with pain, flapping my hand. Watching me jumping around, Bob forgot about his pain. Now we were both richer in experience after this adventure. We were no longer ready to experiment with bees. We returned to observing them dancing in the flower field.

When I got home, my mother was talking to a neighbor about how to get school supplies for me. Since we didn't have money, it worried her very much. Thank God she found out that I could get books and school supplies for free due to our poor economic status. The National Social Services were supporting families like ours. That made my parents very happy. I could not understand why my parents were so excited about getting books for free, but I was happy to see them pleased. The whole procedure for the free books was pretty simple. We needed to fill out the application form, and upon approval, my mother went to pick up the school supplies. She had to wait in line because a lot of families got the books for their children that way, but waiting was not a problem for her. She would have waited even longer if it had been necessary because it was the only way to get the school supplies. I got an old school bag from one of our neighbors. All the preparations for the beginning of school made me overwhelmed, and now with great anticipation and joy, I was waiting for the first day of school.

The orientation day finally arrived. I was very excited. I got up early in the morning at six o'clock, washed my face, had breakfast, and got ready for school. There were many of us from different streets. That day, we were anxious to meet our future teacher. It was Friday, September 1, 1967, my first day at school. My mother took me to school at 7:45 a.m. The school was just a fifteen-minute walk from our house, so we had to leave at that time because first graders started orientation at eight o'clock.

I held my mother's hand tight. I did not know what was waiting for me at school. I just wanted to be with Bob in the same class. We were good friends, so I expected so. On the way to school, I saw a lot of children with their mothers. I also noticed that some children were not happy to go to school. I did not know them. When we arrived at school, we waited in the hallway. The teachers called us by names and took us to the classrooms. Because of the children's noise, I could not understand what was being said. I listened carefully to hear my name. At one point, they called Bob. I wanted them to call me to follow him. Soon afterward, they called me, but I was supposed to go to a different classroom. "Oh no!" I cried to myself. All the mothers had to be in the classrooms while we were meeting our classmates and teachers. I got a female teacher, and Bob did too. Some mothers asked why their children could not be in the same class as their friends from the neighborhood. The teacher replied that it would be better for the children to meet some new children and make new friends.

There were many of us there, and we were confused. I saw some new faces. There were thirty students in each class. It seemed as if we were scared of each other. The teacher explained to the parents and students how we should behave in school. She said we had to be disciplined. At that time, I did not know what it meant to be disciplined. I was quiet and quite withdrawn. I was watching what was happening around me. Some children cried because they were scared. Some of them came with their fathers, some with their mothers.

The class lasted for an hour, but it seemed much longer to me. I did not understand much of what I had seen and heard. When the class finished, the teacher reminded us to come to school with our parents again on Monday. Then we left for home. All the first graders came out of their classrooms, and there was a huge crowd in the hallway. I looked for Bob because I wanted to tell him what the first school day had been like. At that moment, all the children looked alike to me. I only regretted that I couldn't be with Bob in the same class. A crowd of parents and children filled the schoolyard. Some children were looking for their friends, and some were holding their parent's hands and heading home. I finally found Bob. For some time, we talked about our impressions of the first class. We tried to act like heroes, but in fact, we were very scared. At the same time, our mothers were talking about school as well. They were worried about getting everything ready for the school year, but both of us had everything we needed to start school. Bob and I had two more free days to play on the weekend because we knew that after Monday, we would have to focus only on school.

The Branko Radicevic Elementary School, which I attended, is located in the suburb by the main road, which leads to downtown Smederevo. The school was founded in 1946. It was named after one of the most renowned Serbian poets Branko Radicevic, "the poet of youth" as he was and is still known. Branko Radicevic lived and worked in the first half of the nineteenth century. He died of tuberculosis at the age of just twenty-nine. In Serbia, he is regarded as one of the greatest poets of the Romantic Age. Every year on March 28, the school, which I attended, celebrates its anniversary as well as the birthday of this great poet. Not only did I go to this school but also all my brothers and sisters. Their experiences in school were very different. Rick was the worst. He often skipped school and had multiple unexcused absences. He often ran away from both home and school. Because of that, he was placed into a special class intended for children with special needs. I liked my school, although, in the beginning, it was difficult for me to get used to the school rules and to establish a new daily routine. Before I started school, I was free to play with my friends all day long, and now I needed to turn my attention to school, studying, and homework. Bob and I were only a weekend away from the beginning of the school year. The two days went by so quickly as never before.

Monday morning came, the actual first day of school. My mother woke me up at six o'clock. Why so early? I wondered. Since the classes started at 7:30 a.m., my mother calculated how much time I needed to wash my face, get dressed, and have breakfast before school. My bed was too warm and cozy, and I did not want to get up. All of a sudden, I heard my father's voice calling me to wake up. I got up at once. The night before, my mother had packed my schoolbag. I was ready to go, but a problem came up. I had difficulty putting on my shoes. My parents did not have money to buy me a new pair of shoes, so I got some worn shoes from someone that were too tight for me. Somehow, I was able to put them on, and my mother took me to school. On our way to school, I saw that hundreds of parents were taking their children to school, holding their hands. They were pouring from all directions toward the school building like a river flowing quickly to the sea. The school building was new and nicely decorated. With every step we got closer to school, I felt more and more scared. I realized that my fear was just nervousness and anticipation of what was waiting for me and how I would fit in. I tried to get rid of these thoughts, so I decided to take a close look at the children who were to become my classmates. Some of them were trying to pull away from their parents, not wanting to go to school, while others were laughing at the former. I held my heavy schoolbag tight with one hand and my mother's hand with the other. There were so many children in the schoolyard, but I could not see my friend Bob anywhere. "Where is Bob?" I asked my mother.

"He might already be inside," she replied. I had so many questions on my mind walking through the school door. We all entered the big hallway where we took off our shoes and put on the slippers, which we brought from home. All students had to wear slippers in school because some of them lived in villages where the roads were muddy. My slippers were old too, but I did not mind. It was important for me to have them anyway. After changing the shoes in the hallway, my mother took me to the classroom.

According to school regulations, parents attended the beginning of the classes together with their children. My teacher's name was Gilda. She was already waiting for us in the classroom. There were thirty students in my class, including me. With the same number of parents, the classroom was very crowded. You could see right from the start that Gilda was a good teacher. She was very nice to us. After ten minutes, she asked our parents to leave the classroom so that she could get to know us better. That day, we had four classes, and after the classes, our parents were supposed to take us home. Some children did not want to separate from their parents. They started crying while others did not even want to stay. With her friendly approach and soothing words, little by little, the teacher managed to regain control of the situation. The parents left, and there was complete silence. Then the teacher called our names in order to get to know us. After that, she taught us how to sit properly, how to behave in class, how to address adults, and how to show respect to them. It all seemed quite simple and not so new to me. Naturally, there were a few children who were not accustomed to these rules or did not take school seriously enough. The teacher raised her voice, silenced them in no time, and explained the basics of good manners. When I think of my first day at school, I remember listening to the experiences of my older siblings, friends, and neighbors, but my experience was different from anything I had ever heard. I was looking at the faces of my classmates. They reflected fear, confusion, anxiety, and embarrassment, but at the same time, sincereness, friendliness, and excitement. I might have looked the same to them. They reassured me I was not alone. Those faces, which I was looking at that day, are the faces of grown-ups today who are probably dispersed, like by the wind, into the four corners of the world. Whenever I meet any of them, I see the face of a seven-year-old with whom I shared the first great life experience.

Everything looked serious and strict to me at that time—the classroom and desks we were sitting at, the big blackboard I had never seen before, and the teacher. Until then, I did not have time to learn the alphabet. My life was happening outside, beyond the walls, in the green fields, on dusty roads, playing with Bob and other friends of mine. I knew that from that day on, a lot of things were going to change. Since we were not accustomed to being students, the first school day appeared to be too long.

We were expected to sit still and pay attention during all four classes. *It is too difficult*, I thought. The first school day was over. The teacher said goodbye, and we could go to the schoolyard where our parents were waiting for us. As I was changing my shoes and slowly putting my slippers in the bag, lots of words, new rules, and unsorted impressions were echoing in my head. My first impression was that the school was a nice place to which I just needed to adjust to understand it better. Once again, I passed through the long hallway and went out. The noise of the children screaming and laughing could be heard in the schoolyard in front of the school. Many parents were waiting for their first graders. I looked for my mother, but I could not see her. Bob and his mother were nowhere to be found either. All parents left with their children. I was standing there, worried. Obviously, nobody had come to pick me up. I wondered how I was going to get home. I was not sure if I could find the way home, but I had to try. There was no other choice. Some older students noticed me standing alone and started teasing me, "Little first grader, mommy's little baby! Little first grader, mommy's little baby!" It bothered me very much. It was the last thing I needed.

I got out of the schoolyard and turned left. I was sure about that, but the rest of the road was a big mystery for me. Our house was a mile away from school, and I had never used that road before. I tried to recall some details from the morning's walk to school with my mother, but everything around me seemed new and unknown. I was constantly looking back while walking down the sidewalk on the main road. I dreaded the cars, especially the trucks which were honking. I tried to get out of their way as far as I could. I found my way less by memory and more on a hunch. Oh, how happy I was when I saw the old shack and the workers waiting for their bus in the distance. Now I was on familiar ground. At home, I found my mother alone. She was preparing lunch. Doing the housework, she forgot about the time to pick me up. Even the best mothers in the world can sometimes make mistakes. I could not be angry with her. I was proud of myself. It was my first school day, and I managed to come home alone. My overall impression of school was positive. In the beginning, we, the first graders, were shy and a little scared of each other, but in time, as we got to know each other better, beautiful friendships developed among us. First, we practiced handwriting by drawing diagonal, straight, vertical, horizontal, thin, and thick lines in our notebooks. Then we moved on to writing letters. Everything was so exciting and new. The whole world, the world of knowledge, and incredible discoveries were opening up before us. The days were passing by fast.

December came and brought along cold weather. I did not have proper clothes and shoes. I was still wearing light clothes, which could barely be appropriate for the fall, and linen shoes full of holes. Who else would wear them? Probably nobody would. Me neither, but I had no other choice. One

December morning, I was heading to school as usual, around seven o'clock. It was freezing. It was the first frost of the season. I had been going to school alone for some time already. That morning, I felt colder than usual. I hurried to school, trying to avoid the frozen puddles. No matter how hard I tried to watch my step, my torn shoes soon became wet. I arrived at school before my classmates. Oh, how I enjoyed the warmth inside! But I had to do something about the wet shoes and socks. I took them off and put on my school slippers. Then I pulled a chair closer to the radiator and put the shoes on it to dry. I put my feet on the radiator to warm them up and dry my socks. My frozen toes were sticking out through the torn socks. They looked like baby potatoes. My classmates came and saw me drying my torn socks on the radiator. It looked funny to them. They made jokes of my toes sticking out through the holes in my socks. Those were not mean jokes. I laughed with them too. The time to start the class drew near. I had to stop drying my feet. My socks were not completely dry, but they were much more comfortable and warmer than before. As the teacher walked in, she noticed some stirring and giggling in the classroom. She tried to find out what we were laughing about, but my friends did not say a word. They were not malicious, so they did not say anything to the teacher. While I was returning home from school that day, trying again to avoid the puddles, I was thinking about by whom and by what law severe winter had been imposed on Serbia. It was a bad idea, thought the seven-year-old boy.

In the spring of the following year, my father made Marijan's wish come true and bought him a bicycle, a beautiful new shiny bike made in France. At that time, a bike was an expensive item. Our father couldn't have bought it if he hadn't taken out a bank loan. Marijan was thrilled. He was riding and showing off his new French bike everywhere. And the rest of us were happy about the bike too. Marijan would give us a ride around the block almost every day. One day, Marijan was giving Rick a ride around the neighborhood until my mother called them for lunch. Marijan put away the bike, promised Rick to continue the ride after lunch, and went into the house. Rick did not go home but stayed out a little bit longer. He saw Bob, a boy who lived near us. Bob was riding his bike downtown, and he was in a hurry. Rick stopped him and begged Bob to give him a ride to downtown. Bob refused at first, but after a little persuasion, he agreed. Bob's bike was a men's bike, so Rick sat on the horizontal crossbar. They took the steep Partizanska Street. As he was riding down the steep street, the bike chain snapped. This meant that the brakes stopped working. To make it even worse, a big truck was coming toward them. Bob performed a maneuver to avoid a direct collision with the truck. He turned the bike handlebar to the side, and the two of them fell on the street. Rick, unfortunately, bounced and got caught beneath the rear tires of the truck. Seeing that Rick was going to be completely crushed, Bob reacted quickly. He grabbed Rick by the legs and pulled him, trying to save him. He succeeded in that, but Rick's left arm was run over by the truck. The ambulance arrived immediately. Rick was transported to the hospital, but his condition was bad. He was losing a lot of blood. Our parents were informed about the accident and asked to come to the hospital to give their consent to the amputation of Rick's arm. At that moment, the amputation of the crushed arm was urgent and necessary so that Rick would have a chance to survive. My father signed the consent form. It was not an easy decision. The surgery was done. Rick's life was saved, but his left arm was amputated below the elbow. We were all there by Rick's side when he woke up after the surgery. He was in shock and could not accept the fact that he had lost his arm. I felt sorry for Rick.

Unfortunately, this was not the end of the bad news. A few days later, a social worker came to visit us. Rick was registered as a juvenile delinquent, and considering the trauma he had survived, he had no future prospects. Therefore, the social worker suggested sending him to the Juvenile Correctional Institution in Krusevac. The purpose of this measure was to separate him from the company that had a bad influence on him and to give him a chance to learn some craft so that he could support himself later in life. Rick did not like the idea. My father felt sorry for Rick, but he still accepted the suggestion of the social services. Thus, after leaving the hospital, Rick was taken to the Juvenile Correctional Institution.

We did not see Rick for a few years. There was never enough money or the will to go to Krusevac because my father was drunk most of the time.

Sometime when my sister Snezana was around three years old, a local journalist visited us. He set us all in front of the shack in which we lived and took a photo of us. The photo appeared on the front page of the local newspaper with an accompanying story about our poverty and the bad conditions we lived in. As we did not have money to buy the newspaper, one of our neighbors brought it to us to have a look. Overnight, our family became well known throughout the city. You could usually see actors, singers, athletes, and other important and successful people on the front pages, but this time, the photo of our family in all our poverty and misery appeared. I did not feel comfortable about this photo, but the newspaper article caught the attention of the mayor. Moved by the story about our miserable position, he felt responsible for finding us suitable accommodation. There was a quick solution to our problem. Milan, who allowed us to live in his shack, retired and decided to move to Kovin, a neighboring city by the Danube, the second largest river in Europe. The city council decided to let us move into the apartment Milan had been assigned to use, provided that the apartment was under the children's names and not my father's name because my father was too unreliable to be entrusted with the apartment. Our faces were glowing with excitement. We were exhilarated that we were going to move out of the shack and finally live in normal conditions. There was a living room, a bedroom, a kitchen, and a pantry in the apartment. It was not big, but for us, it was a palace.

This is a photo of my parents and Snezana, who was about three years old. It was taken by a friend while we lived in the shack. You can see the fruits and vegetables in our garden that my mother grew.

With the help of our good neighbor, we moved our things to our new apartment. I was not very helpful, but I tried my best. I carried the plates, bowls, pots, and all things my little hands could carry. It was when we moved that I realized how awful the place where we had lived was. The cramped room seemed even smaller to me now. The bricks were sticking out from the walls, everything smelled of alcohol and mold, and not to mention the leaking roof. It is always easy to accept things when they take a turn for the better, so we quickly got used to our bright and cozy new condo. Also, finally, we had electricity.

Unfortunately, the happy days did not last for long. One night, my father came home drunk as usual. He started to scream and make a lot of noise. He woke up the whole neighborhood. The neighbors came and knocked on the door. My father got upset and told them to go home, but they kept knocking on the door. They wanted my father to be quiet so that they could go to sleep because they had to go to work the next morning. Also, they heard that I was crying frantically. They knew my father's aggressive behavior, so they broke down the door. When they entered the apartment, they saw something horrible. My father was holding a knife at my throat. He threatened the neighbors that if they came closer, he would cut my throat. There was a lot of screaming and crying, and everybody was panicking and begging my father not to hurt me. It was a dreadful situation. I just wanted to die so that I would not have to live through this agony ever again. I did not care about my life anymore. My life had been full of fear, and I had no motivation to live. The neighbors tried to calm my father down, but this made him even angrier. This struggle went on for some time. The neighbors tried to get behind him to grab him and take the knife from his hand. My father was pulling my hair with his left hand and holding the knife in his right hand. He knew he was in total control of the situation. Nobody could do anything to stop him. His face became eviler. Finally, as he was turning his face and body toward one of the neighbors, a brave woman quickly pushed him, and he fell down to the ground. The knife fell from his hand, and the woman pulled me away from my father to save me. My father quickly got up and ran out of the apartment. The neighbors stayed with us for a short time, and then they went home. At this moment, I realized what had happened, and terrible fear overcame me. I was trembling like leaves falling from a tree. I was scared to go to sleep, but the exhaustion from fear made me fall asleep. Thank God my father did not come home that night. The next day when he came home, he started to make promises that he would never hurt me again. I had heard his promises so many times before that I did not want to listen to him anymore. Unfortunately, my mom was so fearful of him that she thought she had no other choice but to forgive him. So my miserable life went on as usual.

That summer, an amusement park was set up in a nearby field. A range of amusements, including rides, stalls, and competitions, was available for visitors. There was a huge carousel for grown-ups, a smaller one for children, and a little train circling

along a rail track for toddlers. Young men were showing off before their ladies at the shooting booths
where they tried to win some plastic flowers or soft
toys for their ladies with precise air gunshots at a tin
can. Some men would test their strength with a high
striker. Two riding ponies probably caught most of
the children's attention. There was always a crowd
of impatient children and their parents around the
corral. I liked to ride a pony too. I felt like a real
cowboy in the prairie, proudly riding off into the
sunset. Many people spent pleasant summer evenings
at the amusement park. Sometimes, fights and quar-
rels broke out over the seats on the carousel or when
someone became impatient and tried to skip the line,
but that was not enough to spoil the carnival atmosphere. Barefoot in short pants, without a T-shirt or
a shirt, I made my way through the crowd, trying to
win my portion of fun. I was even "wounded." At
that time, boys did not go anywhere without their
slingshots. Adults made them for the children using
thick wires. One of the projectiles hit me in the bare
back while I was standing by the corral fence watching ponies. I turned around and saw a boy with a
slingshot in his hand and a mischievous grin on his
face. Ouch, it hurt very much! I touched the spot on
my back with my hand, and it was bleeding, and I
thought to myself, *Why is this happening to me?* Not
long after that, the amusement park was going to
close at 10:00 p.m. They would announce the last
ride on the big carousel via loudspeakers and with
the song "Baby, Come Back" by The Equals. They

would finish the program for the day. People were fighting for the last ride with their fists and even with knives, so the police had to intervene. Some people were taken by ambulance due to their injuries. This happened every night before the last ride.

One evening was especially chilly even though it was summer. I hurried home to get warm. The road was passing by blocks of houses, which had separate outhouses. The door of one of the toilets was open. I quickened my pace a few meters away from it. From the corner of my eye, I saw a ghost, a demon standing at the toilet door. I couldn't believe my own eyes. I took a closer look. Surely, it was a demon. It was a silhouette of a triangular-shaped creature with something round like a head on its top. It scared the hell out of me. My bare feet skidded on gravel scattered over the path, leaving a rut as if a truck had passed. I hit my foot on a stone while running, but I didn't feel anything. I did not dare to look back. I just ran. My heart felt like being torn into thousands of pieces with fear, but I kept running as fast as I could, catching my breath. I ran into our apartment, but my parents were not there. Nobody was there. I got even more scared. I turned on the light and grabbed a small ax. My heart was pounding frantically as if I was having a panic attack. I clutched the ax tightly, looking back and listening to every sound. I thought I would not give up without a fight. I would attack the demon with the ax to save my life. Minutes seemed like hours. I could not control my breathing, and my heart was beating like a drum. I do not know how long it took for my parents to arrive, but it seemed forever to me. They found me curled up on the floor, still clutching the ax with my hands. I was holding the ax so tight that the handle of the ax made an imprint in my hand. I told my parents about everything. They were worried. I could not get the image of the demon out of my head for days. Being afraid of what had happened to me that night, I never again returned home late from the amusement park.

Somehow Rick's years in the Juvenile Correctional Institution passed. When he turned eighteen and became an adult, he was released from the institution where he learned to be a house painter. As our father was a house painter, he took Rick as his apprentice. Now father and son started painting houses together. Unfortunately, my father quickly got him into drinking and other vices. Their wages were low, and they spent most of their money in pubs. In the meantime, we added an additional room to our apartment and made it even more comfortable and spacious. As we, the children, were growing, so was the need for expanding our living space.

Rick turned out to be our father's excellent student. He spent more and more time in pubs drinking. One evening, he stayed in a pub until late with Draža, one of his drinking buddies, to help Draža spend his money. Draža lived in Požarevac, a city 20 miles away from Smederevo. As they stayed until very late in the pub, Draža did not have a ride home, so Rick invited him to sleep over at our house. Early in the morning, around six o'clock, my father got up and found Draža sleeping on the mattress on the floor. My father tried to wake him up by offering him a cup of coffee. It was early, and Draža was still feeling hungover and sleepy, so it took him quite some time to get up, according to my father. As my father called his name, Draža was stretching. Who knows what he was dreaming at that moment. All of a sudden, he got half a gallon of cold water on his face. He sprang to his feet immediately, and wet and confused, he asked my father why he had done it. "To wake you up faster," said my father. They both roared with laughter at the "splash" joke. Then they had a little chat over a cup of coffee, and after breakfast, they went to a pub to drink. Draža ended up staying one more night in our house. The next morning, the same wake-up call as the day before was waiting for him, but this time, he was faster than my father, and my father missed him with the water. They laughed together. My father said that Draža was a fast learner. After breakfast, he finally went home.

I have always liked animals, especially dogs. They are honest and unselfish creatures, and I perceive them as our four-legged friends. In some ways, dogs are better than some people. They do not know evil or jealousy, and they would not do anything mean. It doesn't matter to them if you are rich or poor, white or black, a rocket scientist or a simple man. However, they unmistakably distinguish between a good man and a bad one, and once they accept you, you become their best friend forever. Doctors and psychologists nowadays talk about the therapeutic effects of dogs, cats, and other animals on people. This has always been known. The amount of love, tenderness, and emotions that a pet gives to us can naturally develop virtues and boost our physical and emotional well-being.

I was about seventeen years old. It was a snowy winter day. I was walking home down the main street, which divided our neighborhood in two parts. By the fence, right next to the sidewalk, I heard some whining and crying coming from a white nylon bag. It seemed like puppies were crying. I bent down to have a closer look and found a few cute puppies in the bag. They could barely walk. I felt sorry for them. They were too tiny to survive on the street in the cold. I liked one male puppy the most. I decided to take it home. I didn't want to leave the others there either, so I cuddled them all. But there were too many of them to take them all home with me. My heart was breaking. I took my puppy and put him under my coat to warm him up. As I stood up, an old man appeared in front of me. He introduced himself as the owner of the puppies and said that he had watched me cuddling and playing with them. He told me that he had a female German shepherd that had mated with a hunting dog and had delivered a dozen puppies. He was afraid that she would be unable to feed them all, so he decided to get rid of a few so that the rest could have enough milk and a chance to survive. He further told me that he saw how much love and care I had treated the puppies with and that he was moved by my act. Therefore, he decided to return the puppies to their mother and make sure they were properly fed. It was a nice and humane act of the man. He also promised me that the puppy I had chosen would be mine and asked me to wait for a little while until he could grow by his mother's side. I agreed that I would come to check on them every day. And indeed, everything was as we agreed. In order to have enough milk for her puppies, the mother dog was fed more meals and larger portions, and I was delighted to see my puppy and the others grow stronger day by day.

After a month, the puppy, which I named Johnny, became strong enough to be taken home with me. I was floating on air carrying him home. I had planned everything—where to keep him, what to feed him, and how to teach him tricks. I brought him home and poured him a bowl of milk to drink. I knew we did not have enough milk for us, let alone for the dog, but on no account did I want to give up those little shiny eyes and a wiggly tail that tugged at my heartstrings. My whole family was against the dog. They were worried that we could not feed him, but I did not give up. I was determined to keep my Johnny. I took on all the responsibilities with him, and it calmed my family down. Johnny was growing up nicely, and soon he started eating solid food. I got him bones from the neighbors, which he liked the most. I took him along with me everywhere I went. He had his own doghouse in the yard, but sometimes, he would sneak into my bed to cuddle. When he turned one, Johnny became a big, fully grown dog. He was tied with a long chain to the pole of the wired fence next to his doghouse. One night around midnight, a painful whimper came through the silent night quite audibly. I immediately realized that it was Johnny's call for help. I went out and saw an unreal scene. The whole length of Johnny's chain was wrapped around the fence pole, and Johnny was stuck and yowling. It was impossible for him to have done this to himself. It was also impossible for anyone to have done this either. He could have been strangled. The wire fence was tightened on one side of the pole, so there was no reasonable explanation for this situation. I was scared to death, and I suspected it was the work of evil forces. I fell to my knees and prayed. I prayed for Johnny, and I prayed against evil. Suddenly, as if some skilled hands untangled it, the chain fell off the pole, and Johnny was saved. He started barking and jumping around me. I stayed with him for a while, cuddling him until I was completely sure that he calmed down.

When Rick was twenty-one, he met a girl and brought her to live with us. We didn't have enough space for our family, let alone one more person. Their plan was to stay with us until they got married and found a suitable place to live. The evening when Rick's future wife moved in, my father returned home from work drunk. He sat down for dinner when he noticed that somebody was lying on his bed. He came closer and saw an unknown girl sleeping in his bed. He slapped her on the cheek. The girl jumped up in bed. I guess she was still not fully awake when he slapped her on the other cheek. Needless to say, the girl was confused, but my father justified his actions, saying that the girl had allegedly stuck her tongue out at him. Whether it was true or not, Rick's future wife, Ruth, came through her baptism of fire on the very first day with our family. Later, when my father was told who she was, he apologized, but it did not give much comfort to her.

Very soon, Rick and Ruth got married. They had two daughters, and Rick got a job as a courier at the steel plant. The company gave him a brand-new bicycle to ride between factory facilities when delivering mail. Everything would have been nice for Rick and his family if it hadn't been for drinking. Rick was an alcoholic like my father. Hiding from his boss, he regularly drank at work. He earned a decent salary, but he spent most of it at local pubs. This made his family suffer a lot. When he ran out of money, he came up with the idea to sell the bike he used at work. He called a Romani acquaintance of his and sold the bike to him. The next day, Rick's supervisor noticed that Rick had no bicycle at work, and he asked him where it was. "It's been stolen," said Rick. The supervisor immediately reported the theft to the police. Rick was always prone to lying and cheating, and he couldn't be trusted. On the one hand, he lied to his supervisor that the bike had been stolen because he thought that the supervisor would not call the police. On the other hand, the Romani man, like anyone who bought something new, hurried to brag about his new bike to his neighbors, friends, and especially to cute girls. At that time, a bike was an expensive and prestigious thing to have. Not everyone could afford it. Feeling carefree, the Romani man was proudly riding his bike around the city. It did not take long for the police to notice him. Unfortunately, everywhere in the world, as well as in Smederevo, Romani, in general, were labeled as poor people, prone to stealing, cheating, and begging. The same happened this time. The poor man failed to convince the police that he had bought the bike from Rick. The bike was confiscated. He only managed to avoid getting beaten up by the police, but he was left with no money and no bike.

Rick was a very irresponsible man, a cheater, an alcoholic—a carbon copy of my father. Times changed, and people changed. What my mother put up within her bad marriage, Rick's wife did not want to. The two of them soon got divorced. The court concluded that both parents were incapable of performing their parental duties and ordered social services to put the children in a foster home or a home for abandoned children.

In Yugoslavia, all able-bodied adult male citizens had a legal obligation to do military service. Young men were highly motivated to join the military. It was a sign of maturity and masculinity for them. Those who weren't drafted into the army were considered less worthy in society. In November 1978, I received my draft papers. I was supposed to report to the Sombor military base for active duty on January 21, 1979. Sombor is a city in northern Serbia. A lot of my friends and my peers received draft papers as well. The military service lasted for fifteen months and consisted of basic combat training for new recruits and active service for all other soldiers. As many other young men, I was delighted to join the army too. I really liked being a soldier and guarding my homeland. In my country, it was the custom for families to organize a farewell party for their sons joining the army. It was a big party with dozens or even hundreds of guests—relatives, friends, and neighbors who gathered to wish farewells to a young man with music and a feast. On the eve of my reporting to the base, my family organized a big party for me. We celebrated with our guests the whole night. In the morning, my friends saw me off at the bus station. One of them, David, accompanied me to Belgrade from where I transferred to another bus and continued my journey to Sombor.

I arrived in Sombor earlier than requested, so I stopped at a local pub to have a drink and pass the time. Later, at the military base check-in, I took a deep breath, and I showed my draft papers to the duty officer. I met a lot of young men like me there. We were the same age but coming from different parts of the country. In the first few days, we were all confused since the army had its own rules, daily schedules, and especially strict discipline. On the very first day, after breakfast, we were sent to the military barber—not particularly skilled—to cut our hair to meet military standards. It actually meant that they shaved our heads. Instead of wearing civilian clothes, we were given military uniforms. Wearing the same haircut and clothes, we looked the same. We joked, looking at each other, guessing who was actually who.

The first days in the army were busy as we were getting used to military training. After a month, there was a special occasion of taking the oath. By signing the oath, we pledged to protect our homeland and fight for its freedom and honor. It was a solemn act in which all the recruits participated. The recruits' family members, girlfriends or wives, relatives, and friends were also present as guests. Nobody came to see me. I was disappointed, but I had to accept the situation, considering what kind of family I came from. After taking the oath, we were allowed to go to the city, and I went as well. On the first occasion, I took a walk and did some sightseeing in Sombor. Then I had lunch and had my photograph taken to be sent to my family and friends. This was a custom in my country. The next time I was allowed to go out to the city, I picked up the photo from the photographer, and now it is here to remind me of what I looked like as a soldier.

Standard practice of the military authorities at that time was to send soldiers from one republic to another in Yugoslavia to serve in the army. Therefore, after spending two and a half months in Sombor, I got transferred to Vrhnika, a town in Slovenia, where I stayed until the end of my military service. Vrhnika is a beautiful but very small town about 12 miles from Ljubljana. It is known as the birthplace of the great Slovenian writer Ivan Cankar. Slovenia is pretty far from my hometown, so nobody came to visit me. My family did not send me any money either, although sending money to a soldier was a custom so that he could buy something in the canteen or treat himself with something when going out to town. I was not angry with them, although I knew they were able to send me some money as my brothers were employed. I was satisfied with my military pay, which was low, but it covered the costs of shaving accessories, toothpaste, and cigarettes on a monthly basis. Everything else was expected to be provided for a soldier on the military base. Can you imagine my surprise when one day I heard my name over the loudspeakers that somebody had come to visit me? I couldn't believe it. I thought it was a mistake. How glad was I when I saw a well-known face in the reception room! It was Ray, the father of my friend David who had accompanied me to Belgrade and promised me back then that he would come to see me wherever I was. He kept his promise through his father. Ray worked as a driver in the steel plant, and one day, he drove his manager to a business meeting in Ljubljana. After the meeting, he asked the manager to stop by to see me. I was very pleased. The commander granted me a few hours to go out. It was a refreshing change to see a familiar civilian after all the months spent on the military base. He came with his colleagues. We had a pleasant time, and they even treated me to lunch. On parting, we shook hands, and Ray gave me some money, which I gladly accepted. I was sorry that we could not spend more time together, but they were in a hurry, and I had to return to the base.

Life on the base was conducted by strict military rules, but it also had its own so-called "unwritten" rules. One of these unwritten rules was that, even though all soldiers were equal, there was a clear distinction between veterans, nearing the end of their military service, and rookies. Even though I was one of the veterans, I did not like these distinctions, and I could not accept that young soldiers did some of the dirty jobs, such as cleaning the bathrooms, rooms, and the hallways instead of me. I worked with them, giving them an example of equality. I wanted to emphasize that a man should treat others as he wishes to be treated. In order to live in a world worth living in, we must start with ourselves and our own actions.

The happiest day in the life of a soldier is his last day in the army. The night before, I sat with my mates, chatting and having a little fun. We remembered the day we had joined the army and many interesting events during our military service. I also thought about how much we had changed during the last fifteen months. We had come here as bewildered young men, and now we were about to leave as grown-up men, far wiser, and richer in experience. There was a lot of hugging and saying goodbyes to the soldiers who stayed on the base. We comforted them, saying that their discharge time would come quicker than they thought, but at the same time, we regretted to part with the men who had become more than friends to us during our military service. We barely slept that night. The last morning in the army, we spent returning our equipment and weapons. Then we had our last breakfast on the base, and having said goodbye to everybody again, we went to the bus station. We all went together to Ljubljana from where a lot of us took the train to Belgrade. It was a night departure. We were all very happy to be able to go home and hug our loved ones. The train arrived at Belgrade station in the early hours. I could hardly wait for the first bus departure for Smederevo.

It was April 16, 1980. Spring had already come to my hometown, and nature blossomed. All I wanted was to see my family, my dear friends, and my town. I arrived home early in the morning, and my family members were glad to see me. I told them my stories in the army, and they told me what had happened to them while I had been away. The most important news was that I had become an uncle. My sister gave birth to a girl Nancy, who was eight months old when I returned from the army. The girl's father was our neighbor, who refused to acknowledge paternity. Nevertheless, we were happy to have another girl in our family. The neighbors and friends soon found out that I had arrived, and they came to greet me. I told them my stories in the army too. It took me a long time to get rid of my military habits. Sometimes, when I happened to meet an army officer on the streets of Smederevo, I would salute him.

During my absence, my friends had also changed together with their interests. There were some new faces, and some new stories were told. But most of them were my friends, who I knew very well, so it wasn't a problem for me to adjust and continue our friendship. When I returned home from the army, Marijan had the idea of opening a disco club. He invited me to join him in this venture. I liked the idea, so I agreed. The two of us started working together on carrying out the idea. We made a plan and listed all the things we needed. I already had hundreds of vinyl records, and Marijan managed to find all the necessary equipment, which we rented from one of his acquaintances. We had an amplifier, two record players, speakers, a microphone, a light show, and a disco ball as a must-have. During the summer, we were looking for a suitable place so that we could get rolling. We took our business seriously and responsibly. We even printed the club opening flyers and placed them all over the city.

In September, our disco club officially opened in the suburb. Marijan worked as a DJ, and I was the club cashier. We worked three days a week—on Fridays, Saturdays, and Sundays. We sold only soft drinks, and the club soon became one of the most popular places in Smederevo. The club was called

The Doors. More than three hundred visitors came every night. We paid our rent and bills on time every month, and we made decent money. We worked successfully for about six months, and our brother Rick came very often. He enjoyed the atmosphere with lots of beautiful girls, and he was often in the spotlight on the dance floor. Since the accident, Rick had to wear prosthetics attached to his arm with leather straps. He hid it beneath long sleeves so nobody could notice that he actually did not have a part of his left arm. Rick being Rick, never knew to control himself, so one evening, he got carried away by the music and attention of pretty girls and started performing on the dance floor in John Travolta style. Under the dim lights of the disco club, he first took off his jacket and then started unbuttoning his shirt. He wanted to stay in his undershirt only, but while taking off his shirt, his sleeve wrapped around his left arm. Impulsive as he was, he tried to rip it off, but he couldn't. Then he pulled it even harder and pulled his prosthetics off together with his shirt. The prosthetics flew through the air and fell into one girl's lap. In the semidarkness, the girl thought that someone's severed arm fell into her lap. She screamed like hell and scared the people around her. In no time, people started to rush toward the exit. At first, neither Marijan nor I could understand what was going on, but then we saw Rick standing without a shirt and prosthetics, and everything was clear. Disappointed, Marian just asked him, "Dear brother, why have you ruined our disco club?" Having no answer, Rick kept his head down, staring aimlessly at the floor. We knew what the consequences would be, but we hoped that our visitors' trust could be regained.

Unfortunately, our club became infamous, and people no longer wanted to come. The following evening at six o'clock, when we usually opened, only one man came. The man simply had not heard about the incident, so he came to have some fun. He bought a ticket and waited for the other guests. Nobody else showed up. After a while, he stood up, took his ticket, and stuck it on the front door, slamming it behind him. That stuck ticket symbolically marked the last act of our disco club episode. We returned the rented equipment, paid our debts off, and locked the door this time for good.

I had no income, I needed to get a job, but there were no vacancies. My good friend Dragan Stanic offered me a helping hand. I have learned a lot of life lessons from him. He has taught me that you must first respect yourself in order to respect others. His advice has helped me in my life, and I have had an honest and sincere friendship, not only with him but also with his family. As we helped each other, our friendship has grown, and we are still friends. At that time, Dragan worked in our local community office, and he knew the manager of Dunav. He recommended me, and I got a job as a night guard at that company. Dunav was a big company that had its own department store, many self-service shops, several construction material depots, and coal and firewood depots. As night guards, my colleagues and I were armed with guns or rifles. My qualifications for getting this job were that I had completed the firefighter training back in 1978 and that I was a member of the Slavija Volunteer Fire Department. It was significant for my new job because, in case of an emergency, I would know how to react and prevent more serious damage. In Dunav, we had our own fire brigade and fire truck, which I knew how to drive. I was interested in becoming a firefighter, so in June 1982, I finished a course for fire station officers. In Serbia, there were no formal schools for firefighters. There were only courses, equivalent to vocational school programs, organized by the Firefighting Alliance of Serbia. These courses were not easy. They involved serious work and training for future firefighters. I zealously worked at the Slavija Volunteer Fire Department, and I devoted myself to educating the wider population. I realized that ignorance and incompetence of the population were the most common causes of fire. Therefore, at the beginning of the school year, in September 1982, my colleague and I went to see the principal of the Branko Radicevic Elementary School with the idea to start a fire safety course for the students. In the final stage of the course, the children would participate in the Junior Firefighting National Competition.

I was in charge of training the children. The course was attended by children between the ages of seven and fifteen, and they were divided into four teams. We worked with them seriously and studiously, preparing them for the competition. I was in charge of the training, whereas organizational work was done by a man from the firefighting alliance. After qualifying, in October, we went to the national competition, which was held in Pirot. The children were overjoyed that they would represent their school and have a chance to visit Pirot. More than a hundred teams participated in the competition, and we won third place, which was a huge accomplishment. Thanks to the dedicated children, their work, and our God, we managed to rise to such a ranking. Upon our return, the principal was glowing with joy, and the diligent children were rewarded. During that period, I also got a great deal of personal satisfaction from my work. I was honored with the Silver Fire Star, Second Class medal. This medal was awarded not only for showing supreme courage when saving human lives and property but also for dedicated work, as well as special merits in promoting firefighting and fire prevention. By expanding the organization and spreading fire safety awareness among people, with the approval of the city council, we founded the Volunteer Fire Department of Papazovac. We lived in that area, and it was natural to organize ourselves and to do something for our community. People knew I was an honest and hardworking man, and since I had a lot of experience in the fire service, as well as the right qualifications, I was elected to be the chief of the newly formed fire department. In the meantime, I tried to improve myself by attending seminars and courses, and as the culmination of years of practice and hard work, I passed the license exam to be a fire chief.

This is a photo of me as the chief of the
Volunteer Fire Department of Papazovac
in Smederevo, taken in 1982.

ВАТРОГАСНИ САВЕЗ СРБИЈЕ

додељује

ДИПЛОМУ

Ивић Денис

као знак признања II степена, којим је, на основу одлуке председништва Ватрогасног савеза Србије, одликован за пожртвован рад и нарочите заслуге на унапређењу ватрогаства и заштите од пожара

Секретар

Бр. 612/1 Београд 07.10.1982

Председник

THE FIREFIGHTERS ASSOCIATION OF SERBIA

CONFERS THE

DIPLOMA

TO

IVIC DENIS

IN RECOGNITION OF II DEGREE WITH WHICH, BASED ON THE DECISION OF THE PRESIDENCY OF THE FIREFIGHTERS ASSOCIATION OF SERBIA, HE IS DECORATED FOR HIS DEDICATED WORK AND EXCEPTIONAL CONTRIBUTION TO THE IMPROVEMENT OF FIREFIGHTING AND PROTECTION AGAINST FIRE

THE SECRETARY

[HANDWRITTEN SIGNATURE]

NO. 612/1 BELGRADE, 10.07.1982

[illegible stamp]

THE PRESIDENT

[HANDWRITTEN SIGNATURE]

This is my Silver Fire Star, Second Class medal with the accompanying diploma from 1982. I have never paid too much attention to my awards. I have considered them only a motivation to work even harder and to improve both myself and the community I belong to. I used to think like that, and I will continue to believe in it for the rest of my life no matter where I am.

The following year, in 1983, the national competition was held in Bajina Basta. It is a picturesque and welcoming town with only a few thousand residents about 120 miles south of Smederevo. I have to say that the firefighting competitions were not very popular, so we had problems with getting money for the trip. About forty children and ten adults were supposed to go to the competition. Unfortunately, the city council did not have money to finance the trip. The accommodation was arranged with the help of the competition organizer. We agreed that the children would be accommodated in the homes of their peers from Bajina Basta. We still needed to find the money necessary for the trip. A few of us tried to convince some large companies in Smederevo to help us. Unfortunately, they all refused. At the last moment, to our great delight, Dragan Stanic was able to help us. The agricultural company Godomin offered to give us their bus and driver for the trip. Needless to say, we were disappointed that the city of Smederevo, with a population of one hundred thousand people and strong business entities, with the exception of Godomin, did not want to help us. It is said that the road to success is covered by thorns, but those who bear hardships will be successful. Once everything was settled, the parents gave the consent for their children, and we were ready to set off. The competition was scheduled to start on Friday, May 22, and end on Sunday, May 24, when our return to Smederevo was planned. We had both male and female teams to compete with children under twelve and in cadet categories. Several members and the president of the Papazovac Fire Department went along. My sister Snezana, who in the meantime finished the firefighting course and worked as a security guard at the company Velur in Smederevo, joined us together with her friend Sladjana, some of her classmates, and my neighbors. On our departure day, many parents came to see us off. The children were looking forward to the trip, and the caring parents filled the children's bags with some snacks for them to take. I lined the children up, like little soldiers, by calling their names one by one to get on the bus. When we all got on the bus, the parents waved and wished us a safe journey. Our driver Pera honked, and we set off for Bajina Basta. The children were cheerfully singing, talking, and enjoying the trip. They were really good children.

Bajina Basta welcomed us with streets decorated with firefighting symbols. The whole town was in the spirit of the upcoming competition. Everything was impeccably organized. Our children were welcomed with open arms by their friends and kind hosts who were to accommodate them for the next few days. All of us, the adults, could not afford a hotel room, so we slept on gym mats at the local school while the hosts provided meals. We didn't mind such accommodation. We came to Bajina Basta in good spirits in order to compete, have fun, meet new people, and make friends. The competition consisted of two parts. First, the children had to take tests. They had to answer one hundred questions in sixty minutes. The second—practical part—was done on a large football field. The children had a task to put out a fire using a fire extinguisher while the cadets simulated pumping water out of a flooded basement using an electric water pump. All of them did a great job. Friday and Saturday were reserved for elimination rounds and Sunday for the finals. As our children successfully completed the tasks, it was clear that we were among the favorites, but other teams were also good. There were a lot of teams from all over Serbia. We also had enthusiastic fans. All of us, supported by the host children, cheered loudly. We almost lost our voices by the end of the day. Sunday came. We made it to the finals and were eager to start the last day of the competition. Our teams received a lot of support from the fans. The host children cheered louder for us than they did for their own hometown! We spared neither our voices nor our hands. The teams completed their tasks, and now it was up to the judges to calculate the points and announce the winners. The national competition winner announcement was scheduled to begin at 1:00 p.m. The winner was the home team because the judges were biased. We won third place. A little injustice was done to us, but there was nothing we could do about it. Some of the children cried, but winning third place in such a big competition was a remarkable success. After the medal ceremony was held, the children had lunch and said goodbye to their hosts. Some beautiful new friendships were built during our stay. It was hard for the children to leave, but they exchanged addresses so that they could keep in touch. In the afternoon, we set off for Smederevo with the medals in our hands as proof that we were worthy of attention and that the city council and the local companies should have supported us. On the way home, the atmosphere on the bus was cheerful. The children sang songs and told funny stories. Only the seven-year-olds, the first graders, dozed off due to the long trip and the excitement of the days.

We arrived in Smederevo in the late afternoon. A lot of parents and our friends were waiting outside the school gates. As the bus was approaching, many parents were waving impatiently to see their children. The children got off the bus in orderly fashion. They were wonderful children. I never had a single problem with them. They ran into their parents' arms excitedly, telling them what a wonderful time they had in Bajina Basta and boasting about their success. I left our third-place trophy at the Volunteer Fire Department of Papazovac, and a lot of people from the department congratulated all of us, especially me, for my hard work in training them. I thanked my colleague, Slavko, for helping me with the training. The next few days, I received compliments and congratulations from the principal and teachers of the Branko Radicevic Elementary School. The story of our success became widely known, so messages of congratulation came from everywhere—not only from the community, city council, mayor, and then chief of police, but also from friends and acquaintances. I must admit I enjoyed these compliments and congratulations. I perceived them as encouragement and support for my future work with children. The biggest support came from the local community and my friend Dragan Stanic. He arranged transportation for our trip. He supported us in all our endeavors. He is a good and honest man, an example of what a friend should be. As the end of the school year was coming closer, we suspended our activities until September.

In agreement with the school principal, in September, we continued working with the children in our firefighting club. We trained on Saturdays and

Sundays in the schoolyard, preparing for the competition that was supposed to be organized in Novi Sad the following spring. The children practiced unrolling a fire hose, working with different couplings, manifolds, and nozzles, as well as attaching a hose to a fire hydrant. We also trained them to work with electric water pumps and fire extinguishers. All the equipment was usually stored at the local fire station close to the school, and the children had to carry them to the schoolyard for every session and then return them to the fire station after the training. The transfer of the firefighting equipment caught the attention of curious passersby, who wanted to know why we carried the equipment, and they started mocking the children. I advised the children not to pay attention to people's comments but just to look ahead, work hard, and strive for their goals. The children in the club were divided into groups according to their age. The younger ones practiced using simple equipment, and the older ones, the cadets, worked with water pumps and complex fire extinguishing systems. The children really enjoyed what they were doing, which meant a lot to me. They also felt worthy because they were doing an important and responsible job reserved for adults only. The local community could not finance us, so I often bought refreshments for the children after a hard training. Sometimes, I even brought them biscuits or sweets. They worked hard, and I wanted them to feel comfortable, so I treated them with some small treats. I did not mind spending my own money because I enjoyed working with them. We met every weekend until the cold weather hit. Then we stopped training outside during the winter, and we worked inside on acquiring theoretical knowledge of firefighting. The national competition awaited us in the spring.

At that time, I worked as a night guard at Dunav Trade. During the winter, the job of a night guard was especially difficult not only because of the bad weather but also because of the thieves who were particularly interested in the coal brought in railroad cars. If they had managed to steal it, they would have sold it in baskets around the city to be used for heating homes. Due to a high volume of work and additional danger, we worked on the night shift in pairs. We were armed. After I got a firearms license, I obtained a Zastava 7.65 mm caliber handgun. My colleagues carried rifles. We often confronted thieves at night. They were mostly Romani armed with knives, axes, and especially dangerous daggers, which they made from metal files. I had to fight with these thieves every night. I had been trained in karate and enjoyed fighting, so it was not a big deal for me. When we caught the thieves, we turned them in to the police for further action. Doing this job was not easy at all. Some of my colleagues were afraid of frequent confrontations with the thieves. I wasn't afraid, perhaps because I had a lot of experience with violence due to my father's abuse when I was little. These problems were nothing compared to the troubles with my father. My colleagues loved to work with me on the same shift. We guarded the railroad cars, which were often parked on several station tracks. We skillfully wriggled through and under the railroad cars in order to secure them. I had compassion for the poor Romani people who could not afford coal for the winter. I allowed them to pick up all the coal that fell off the trains during the transfer, but I could not allow them to steal from the railroad cars. People in town also liked me because many times, I protected children and women from bad people. When I caught these bad people trying to hurt the children and women, I simply beat them up. I could not stand violence against weak and vulnerable people. I remembered very well how my father had hurt me, so I decided that I would not let bad people hurt others.

With the first days of spring and nice weather, we continued our firefighting training with the children. We were hastily preparing for the competition, which was scheduled for May in Novi Sad. It was our third year competing. We were more experienced and well known for our achievements all over Smederevo, so it was easier than before to find sponsors for our upcoming trip to Novi Sad. Everything was like the previous year. The company Godomin gave us their bus and driver, thanks to my friend Dragan Stanic. We were accommodated in the homes of our kind hosts, and again, we took third place. It seemed like we were subscribed to the bronze medal. The roar of the crowd might have subconsciously influenced the judges to rule in favor of the home team again. Nevertheless, it was a great success that we took third place out of one hundred teams. Even the following year, when the competition was held in Jagodina, we took, as you can guess, third place again. But in 1985, we hosted the competition. The children trained hard on the weekends, and the result was outstanding. We didn't have too much time to train, but we won first place and the competition trophy. You can't imagine how the children squealed with joy. They won all events. Besides the trophy, they were provided with appropriate firefighter uniforms, which especially delighted them.

This is a picture of me with all
our junior firefighters.

That year, by the rules of the fire department, I was supposed to be promoted to the rank of first-class subofficer. The rank is obtained, by the rules of the service, after four years of devoted work in the fire brigade. My colleague Nate, who also expected a promotion, was supposed to send the necessary documents, i.e., the proposals for the promotion, to the Firefighting Alliance of Serbia, but he did not do it. The two of us worked together at the fire department of Papazovac. Jealous of my work with the children and the fact that the people in the community appreciated and loved me, he made a glaring omission and failed to send the proposal for my promotion. However, he did not forget to send the proposal for his own promotion. I am not recalling this because of a missed rank but because of the lesson I learned. Not all people show solidarity for others or are ready to participate in the success of the society and the community they belong to. There are always those who are selfish and envious and for whom other people's success is their own failure. Due to this conflict, the fire department was suffering. Nate took charge of the fire department, but since the community did not support him and the members of the alliance did not like him, the firemen of the department started to leave, and the fire station soon had to close down.

In the spring of 1986, I had my first contact with the Seventh-day Adventist Church. My brother's friend Ljubodrag Cirkovic recommended us to go to the evangelistic series, which were held in Smederevo. Evangelization is the act of spreading the good news, the gospel of Jesus Christ. Marijan attended a Bible study with his friend and then stayed for dinner at Pastor David Adamovic's house. During that period, Marijan had constant headaches, but after that evening, his headaches stopped. Marijan continued to visit Pastor David. They studied the Bible, and the pastor taught him about a healthy vegetarian diet. On August 14 of that same year, our father died after a long and serious illness. He was visiting his relatives in Kosovo when he passed away from lung cancer. At his own explicit wish, we buried him in Kosovo, his birthplace.

Marijan kept inviting me to go to church with him, but I was skeptical. I was not familiar with the Adventist Church. Thanks to my mother, I knew a little about the customs and beliefs of the dominant Orthodox Church, although I had never visited a church before. However, the existence of other churches was unknown to me. Marijan was persistent in his endeavor to bring me to the Adventist Church. A couple of times, Pastor David sent his regards and invitations to me by Marijan. In the fall, I made peace with Nate. People say it is human to forgive. I am not a quarrelsome man, and I wanted to be at peace with myself and everybody around me, so I forgave and made peace with Nate. I didn't know that he knew Pastor David Adamovic too. He convinced me that Pastor David was a good man and suggested that the two of us should visit him together.

At that time, my job as a night guard had quite an impact on me. Frequent confrontations with thieves, responsibility at work, and hard work on the night shift made me drink more and more. I did not let other people see me drunk, and unlike my father, I was not violent. I actually despised aggression, and I was particularly bothered by violence against weaker people. In such situations, I would always take the side of the victims. Several times I even got into fights with bullies in order to protect the victims from them. This personality trait of mine to stand up to injustice and violence probably stems from my childhood traumas.

Having heard so many nice words about Pastor David and the church, I accepted the invitation to meet him. It was in the fall, in October when Pastor David kindly invited Nate and me to his home. Since my work shift started at 6:00 p.m., we agreed to visit him around 4:00 p.m. Pastor David lived with his family in the same building where the church was. I met Nate, and we headed to the pastor's home. It was a chilly fall afternoon. As we were walking along the street, I had no expectations, just a lot of confusing questions. We quickly arrived, Nate rang the doorbell, and David Adamovic opened the door. David was a decent and respectful man. He greeted us warmly as if we had known each other for years and showed us in. As we were taking off our coats in the hall, the pastor's cheerful children—seven-year-old Jovan and six-year-old Jasmina—came running to say hello and brought us slippers to make us feel at home. A sudden rush of warmth and emotions overcame me. I have met some good and honest people in my life, but Pastor David is an example of nobility, and with every gesture, every word of his, he showed respect to people. The children were so nice that they looked to me more like characters from a fairy tale like they were not of this world. We sat comfortably and started a conversation. David was interested in my life, where I worked, what I did, and what my plans for the future were. I could see that he knew some things about me from Nate and my brother's stories, but he was surprised when I told him about the dangers I was facing all the time in the workplace. Then we moved on to religious topics. It was only by listening to the pastor that I realized how little I actually knew about God and how poor my knowledge was when it came to that subject. While we were talking, the pastor's wife, Ljiljana, was preparing dinner. I was embarrassed to stay for dinner and tried to find a way to excuse myself and leave. The pastor noticed my discomfort and insisted that Nate and I should stay for dinner. Even the children asked us not to leave. Never before had I felt so honored and respected, so I couldn't refuse them. The time flew by while we were talking and having dinner. I had to hurry in order not to be late for work. Walking from the pastor's home to the depot where I worked, I couldn't stop thinking about him, his family, and his words. Things started to take shape in my head after this visit. For a long time that night, I was thinking about the love and attention that the family showed me by letting a complete stranger into their home and hearts. And I also let them into mine forever.

It was a turning point in my life. I made friends with the pastor's family and started visiting them regularly. I realized that they not only spoke the Word of God but also lived according to it, which I particularly liked. I started studying the Bible with Pastor David. Every time I went to study with him, I put my gun in the drawer out of respect to God. My sincere wish to understand God's will and Word led me to the study of the Holy Scriptures. I was thrilled as I was reading the pages of the Bible with a humble spirit of a learner who wanted to know what the Bible said. I met other people who attended the Adventist Church. They were all good Christians. No one ever forced me to do anything. Things took their natural course, and after four months of studying the Bible, I wished to be baptized. I was ready to accept Christ as my Lord and Savior and become a follower of Him.

This is my mother and me from the period before I met Pastor David. You can clearly see how terrible I looked. My body depleted by alcohol looked like an empty shell. My mother is sitting next to me. The fifty-five-year-old woman looked like an eighty-year-old grandma. The consequences of her miserable life could be seen on her face. All the things our father did to her left an indelible mark on her.

I did not leave my vices. I still fought on the streets every day. Fighting was like an addiction to me. When I wasn't fighting, I was shaking just as much as an alcoholic would shake from the alcohol withdrawal symptoms. Every time when my friends told me that there was fighting somewhere in the city, I ran to the spot like other people would hurry to celebrate a wedding. I also smoked cigarettes and drank alcohol. These passions were stronger than my virtues. I was absolutely obsessed with the idea of drinking. It seemed as if someone else had control over my mind. In the morning, after waking up, I immediately lit a cigarette and took a few shots of cognac, savoring its flavor as it easily slid down my throat. On my right hand, some of my fingers had small dark brown spots. I woke up one morning and reached for a cigarette. I lit it, but it had an unpleasant, unbearable smell. I threw it away and lit another one, but it smelled bad too. I threw that away and took another one again. It tasted and felt disgustingly awful. I thought there was something wrong with that pack of cigarettes, so I opened a new one, but everything was the same. I was repulsed by the cigarettes, and I couldn't stand their smell. I took a big sip of coffee and spat it out right away. Then I reached for some cognac to clear my throat, but the smell of it made me want to puke. I was utterly confused about what was happening to me. Later that day, when I saw Pastor David and told him what had happened to me that morning, he just smiled. He told me that everyone in the church had been praying for me over the past three months to quit all addictions—coffee, cigarette, and liquor. That was a true miracle from God. From that moment on, I left all the vices behind me and started a new life to live uprightly in holiness before God and in accordance with His laws.

Preparations for my baptism were well underway, so I informed my closest friends. The reactions were mainly positive. However, one of my colleagues

thought I was crazy to choose to be baptized. I realized that he did not like this idea because he knew
I would not drink alcohol with him ever again. I
scheduled my baptism for April 18, on my birthday.
The date would symbolically represent not only the
day when I was physically born but also the day of
my spiritual rebirth. In 1987, it fell on a Saturday, so
the symbolism of the date was even more significant
since Saturday is the seventh day of the week, which is
the Sabbath of the Lord, according to the Bible. The
fourth commandment says that we are not supposed
to work on the Sabbath. Unfortunately, my manager's approach showed a complete misunderstanding
of my situation. He refused to give me Saturday off.
Whether he had something against the Adventist
Church or me, or he was just intolerant by nature.
I don't know, but he did not want to give me a day
off on Saturday. Pastor David also tried to help me.
We went together to see my manager, hoping that we
would convince him to give me Saturday off, but in
vain. He didn't even want to listen to David. Then he
became angry and threatened me, saying that while
he was in charge, I would not get Saturdays off. I had
already had enough of my lousy job, and right there,
I gave my resignation to him. I did not want to let
him stand in my way to God. The manager instantly
changed his mind and started persuading me not to
quit, saying that he needed me and that I was the best
employee. But I stuck to my principles. This happened three days before my baptism.

I was determined to fight for my rights at any cost, for the right to freedom of conscience and freedom to serve my God. I want to tell you this: If you feel the presence and guidance of the Holy Spirit, do not hesitate, but hold on to His hand and take the path of life our Creator has made known to us in the Bible. I have heard of stories about people who were afraid of losing their jobs or some other benefits because of following the Word of God. You should not be afraid or have doubts. There are no uncertainties or risks if you fully trust the Lord. In His word, God committed to men the knowledge necessary for salvation, and the Holy Scriptures are to be accepted as an authoritative, infallible revelation of His will. Jesus died on the cross for our sins and purchased our salvation. He conquered death through His resurrection and promised to return and take us home to the kingdom of heaven. The Bible is like a detailed map which clearly directs us on the way to heaven. All we have to do is surrender our hearts, our bodies, and our minds and follow Him.

Preparing for my baptism, I abandoned my wrong beliefs and habits. I felt as if I was reborn as if I was given a new life. And the day came, Saturday, April 18, 1987, the day of my solemn covenant of complete obedience to God. I was baptized by being immersed in water in the name of the Father and the Son and the Holy Spirit. I can honestly say that it was like a miracle. I was immersed in water, and I came out as a new person, spiritual and filled with love. I even got the baptismal verse from the epistle of Paul: "Fight the good fight of the faith, lay hold on eternal life, whereunto thou art also called, and hast professed a good profession before many witnesses" (1 Timothy 6:12). The pastor of the Smederevo church, David Adamovic, baptized me. Many members of the church, such as Zorica Lužajić, Ljubodrag Ćirković, Lilja Adamovic, and my mother witnessed my baptism. A lot of them knew what my life had been like before I got to know Jesus. They congratulated me on my baptism and the changes I had made in my life. Many of my Orthodox and atheist friends noticed that I had changed and congratulated me too. In the past, I often picked fights, drank a lot, and had an unhealthy lifestyle, but praise God because He called me out of the darkness and led me on the right path, the path of righteousness. After finding the Lord, everything changed in my life. I left all my vices in the past. I led my life in accordance with the Bible and adopted some Bible verses as my new life principles.

From the epistle of Paul, it says, "I can do all things through Christ which strengthens me" (Philippians 4:13).

And from Solomon's Song that celebrates human love, it says, "Many waters cannot quench love; neither can the floods drown it: if a man would give all the substance of his house for love, it would utterly be contemned" (Solomon's Song 8:7).

The Lord loves me the way I am. I believe with all my heart that He is my personal Savior. He, the Creator of all things, knows me, enlightens my path, and removes obstacles. God has given me the guidelines for holy living. He expects me to follow Him, and He will support me in everything I do. I have learned in life that you should do good both to those who are good to you and to those who aren't. Stay away from the wicked and from those who do you harm.

Since I had resigned, I had no job, so I decided to look for happiness abroad. I was given the opportunity to go to Austria to work. My brother Marijan was already in Vienna. He lived and worked there, so he let me stay with him and found me a job. Pastor David gave me the address of the Adventist Church in Austria, advising me to contact them if I needed any help. It was Sunday, June 8, 1987, when I set off for Vienna. As previously agreed, the driver drove me to Marijan's apartment, which was in the twelfth district. It was a pleasant journey of about ten to twelve hours. The driver literally drove me to Marijan's door, and Marijan paid him for the ride. The next day was my first day at work. I got a job as a construction worker, working on building facades. Yugoslavia, as a state, still existed at the time. There was no hatred among people on the basis of nationality in Austria, and people called all of us from Yugoslavia "Jugovici" after the country's name. We were all friends, and we helped each other in good and bad times. Those were the good old days!

Marijan and I lived in a very old building where there was no shower in the bathroom. We had to go to a public bathroom to take a shower. On

Fridays, I prepared meals for the next day because we, Adventists, keep the Sabbath, and we do not do any kind of work on Saturdays. We spend all day in church to study the Bible. According to the Word of God, the Sabbath is a holy day, a day that we dedicate to God. It was my first Saturday in Vienna. The two of us took a tram to church. Marijan left after the sermon, and I stayed in church all day long. I did not speak German, nor was I familiar with Vienna, so returning home was a problem because I had to transfer from one tram to another. Thanks to God, I managed to find my way back to the apartment.

Over time, I got to know people who regularly came to the Adventist Church, and I found them all to be good people with whom I gladly spent time. When we finished our work on the building facade we were working on, I had no job again. I made money to pay the rent and buy food by doing odd jobs, mostly with my fellow countrymen "Jugovici." Nobody wanted to hire me because I didn't speak German. Then a man I met at the Adventist Church, Victor, had his own company and gave me a job there. I started working with Walter, a Serbian man, on demolishing an old building and clearing the construction site. I remember when I first went to work by tram. I had the address, but I did not know how to get there. I turned to the tram driver and showed him the address. He was a kind man. I didn't speak German, and he didn't speak Serbian, but we understood each other by eye contact, without any words. I was grateful to him. In my life, I have met a lot of nice people who have made me a better person. Kindness is a wonderful human trait, something most amazing on earth. I feel that all human beings on this planet are God's children connected to each other. And therefore, I would like to thank all the people that I had contact with for their kindness. I want to pass the goodness on to others by being good to everybody.

We worked on clearing the construction site till the end of the year. When the construction season finally came to an end, I decided to take a break and travel to Serbia. Marijan stayed in Vienna so that we could keep the apartment. I stayed in Serbia for two months. I visited my friends and spent some time with my mother and relatives. In February, the break was over, the construction season continued, and I returned to Austria. Victor offered me a job again. He was a good man. We hung out together and became very good friends. His family often invited me for lunch on Saturdays. He, his wife, and two sons were a lovely family.

I attended the Adventist Church regularly and was actively involved in their activities. I met a lot of people, and I had a wonderful time with them. During the summer, we had Bible studies in nature. We all brought food and ate there together. I took my camera on one of these trips, and so this photo was taken.

When I took a look at myself in the photo, I was surprised to see how much I had changed during that year, for the better, of course, a year of a healthy life, vegetarian diet, no vices, and above all, a year spent in humble devotion to God. The changes improved my life tremendously. I even wrote two songs in praise of God.

Star
By Denis Ivic

One more day as night was falling
I darkness, in darkness
The Star was shining
One more day as night was falling
In darkness, in darkness

The Star was shining
Will the day tell the night
Why the Star had to disappear
How sad it sounds, to say that
Why the Star had to disappear
The moment the stone was
moved from the grave
Why the Star had to disappear
The moment the stone was
moved from the grave
The Star was shining, the Star
was shining
The Star was shining, the Star
was shining
The Star was shining

Sorrow
By Denis Ivic

On my heart sorrow falls
It falls and rolls around
Why don't you stop this blind
sorrow
Can't you see it's the end of the
world
On my heart sorrow falls
It falls and rolls around
Why don't you stop this blind
sorrow
Can't you see it's the end of the
world

You're heading to the cold grave
But I have the Redeemer of this
world
There is joy in my heart
That Christ died for this world
You're heading to the cold grave
But I have the Redeemer
There is joy in my heart
That Christ died for this world

Since my mother saw the big difference that Christianity brought to my life, she became interested in the Bible too. She started to study the Bible with Zorica Luzajic, and she was baptized by Pastor David Adamovic on March 31, 1989, two years after my baptism. I was thrilled that my mother became a believer. In the Adventist Church, members are baptized by full immersion in water. This was a big challenge for my mother because she was scared of water since she had almost drowned at the age of twelve. It was a real miracle that she got over her fear of water and was able to be baptized by immersion. Everybody in church was aware of this and was excited to witness her baptism. My mother was very happy to start her new Christian life, and her faith grew day by day.

In 1991, our brother Rick came to Vienna too, searching for a better life and true happiness. Unfortunately, that year will be remembered by our family for a painful event, the loss of our mother. After our father passed away, our mother lived alone in an apartment, and we, her children, went on our way to look for happiness. On October 2, she got sick and was rushed to the hospital. My sister Gina got a call from the hospital, saying that our mother was seriously ill. The same night I heard from Gina, I set off for Smederevo, Serbia. I paid a man to give me a ride to Smederevo. I remember the music that was on the radio all the way. The other passengers enjoyed the trip, but I cried. I couldn't hold back my tears, and I couldn't stop worrying about my mother. The driver drove me to the hospital in Smederevo. I ran inside and tried to find out from the doctors on duty where and in what condition my mother was. I found her lying in bed, unconscious in the intensive care unit, on life support. I sat by her side for a long time, massaging gently her cold feet and tired hands. I was looking at my poor mom, who sacrificed her whole life for her children. She endured years of beatings from her husband. She was starved and tortured, and now in the hospital bed, she seemed so serene. Her roommate looked at me and said, "If your mother could see you now, she would get well."

"If it was possible, I would give her all the love in the world, just to get better," I replied. That afternoon, I paid a visit to my mother in the hospital again. I wanted to spend as much time as possible with her. The next day, I visited her with my sisters Gina and Nance. Gina came with her two children and Nance with one of her good friends. To avoid making too much noise and disturbing other patients in the hospital room, we agreed to have Nance and her friend come in first and then the rest of us.

She came out of the room in a minute and told us that Mother wasn't looking good. We went inside, and I tried to feel my mother's pulse, but in vain. I called the nurse and the doctors, but unfortunately, they could only pronounce our mother dead. This wonderful woman, a warm person, our dear loving mother passed away quietly during our visit. I stood comfortless. Tears flooded uncontrollably down my face. Organizing the funeral for the next day, I couldn't stop crying. Marijan, Rick, and our sister Snezana came from Austria. A lot of people attended our mother's funeral. My friends from church organized a lunch in the church for everyone. Afterward, Pastor David made a speech on the second coming of Christ, adding that everyone who lived righteously would be with Jesus in the kingdom of God forever (Revelation 21:1–4).

After our mother's funeral, I took advantage of an opportunity in Serbia and bought the apartment where my mom lived from the state. I told Gina and her family to move in so that they would not have to pay rent anymore. I went back to Vienna, and I lived there with my sister and brother until 1995. We lived on beautiful Rosas Gasse Street near Schönbrunn Palace. This baroque palace, with its marvelous architecture, was the main summer residence of the Habsburgs, the Austro-Hungarian emperors. Schönbrunn is not just a palace. Its vast gardens are an oasis in the city center. I often visited this palace with my friend Goran Petronijevic and my family to get away from the hustle and bustle of the city.

Here is a photo of me in Schönbrunn Park.

Our Rosas Gasse Street was very beautiful, full of greenery and roses. Maybe you can't see the roses clearly because of so much greenery. This is one of my favorite photos taken in this beautiful garden between the buildings. I have great memories of Vienna, one of the most beautiful cities in Europe.

In Vienna, I could not get a work permit, so I had to go back to Serbia. Upon returning to Serbia, I worked as a photographer. I photographed weddings, children's birthday parties, and other special events and occasions. I did it for two years, and then, together with Peter, I invested some money in the production of facade stones, fountains, jardinieres, concrete statues, columns, garden pavers, and other concrete ornaments.

This picture shows some of the things I made in this business.

Although I was very busy with work, God was always in my heart. I will never forget how He has changed me and made me a better man. He is here with me every day and shows me what is important in life. The Bible makes it clear—don't follow the wisdom of the world, but follow the wisdom of God, and don't worry about your life. My promise to God is summed up in a wish to be "a good branch in the vine" (John 15:5).

In those years, Serbia was again in a political and financial crisis, so my friend Noah and I decided to look for a better life abroad. We packed some necessary things and set off for Hungary. We arrived in Budapest at about 2:00 or 3:00 a.m. and went straight to a modest but neat and comfortable hotel to sleep. In the morning, after taking some rest from the ride, we went to the Adventist Church, hoping to get some help. There we met Daryl, who sent us to the Adventist Center in Pecel. Noah accompanied me to Pecel, and then he continued his journey to Vienna, Austria. Pecel is a small town in the northern part of Hungary some 18 miles away from the city where the Adventist Theological College and campus are located. I was accepted at the Adventist Center. I shared a room with Paul, a man from Serbia. There were other people from Serbia there, like a nice lady Jen, who was staying there with her son. The college secretary did everything that was necessary for my residency registration. I was registered at the college address. We got along with each other pretty well and organized our lives on the campus. The nearest store was a mile away, so sometimes, it was hard to carry all those heavy grocery bags and other supplies. We all cooked on one stove, so we made a schedule, trying to give priority to Jen, being a woman with a child.

On the very first Saturday, I joyfully headed to Budapest and the Adventist Church, which was located on Szekely Bertalan Street. I was glad to see my friend Daryl and his family again. There were some other Serbians there too. As none of us spoke Hungarian, we gathered together and studied the Bible in Serbian. Dragana and Zoran Meseldzija joined us. I met these wonderful people for the first time and became friends with them right away. This is one of the situations where you meet someone and have the feeling that you have always known each other. The sincere and deep friendship which was born then continues to this day.

There are few people, despite a large number of friends I have made in my life, with whom I have built such deep connections. I can safely say that I have learned a lot from them. Dragana and Zoran are also Adventists, true Christians who live in accordance with the Bible.

Budapest is a beautiful city. I carried my camera with me all the time, and I took pictures of the attractions. This picture shows the famous Chain Bridge.

This is the picture of Heroes' Square that I took. This is another historical landmark of the city.

In the beginning, I did not have a job in Budapest, so I spent most of my time walking around the city, taking pictures. On Saturdays, I regularly went to church on Szekely Bertalan Street, where I met a lot of nice and interesting people, but I spent most of my time with the Meseldzija family. They lived in Budapest and worked in book publishing. They did their work on the computer, so thanks to them I had my first contact with a computer. They created an e-mail account for me, and I wrote e-mails to some people whose e-mail addresses I knew. Two days passed without any response. When on the third day, no one replied. I admit I felt a bit disappointed. My friends seemed to have noticed that. The next day, I visited them, and as usual, I asked Zoran to check my mail. Everything was the same, except that my friends were smiling at me. I paid no attention to it. We turned the computer on and viola! There was an e-mail in my inbox. I was very pleased, and I started bragging to Dragana. She just smiled and excused herself, saying that she had some urgent work to do in the kitchen. Nothing seemed suspicious to me. I opened the e-mail, and it all became clear to me. Seeing how impatient I was to start digital correspondence, my friends decided to play a joke on me by writing an e-mail to me. We all laughed, but at the same time, I was glad that I had received my first e-mail from my dear friends.

The management of the campus we lived on informed us that from September, we would have to pay $180 for rent. I didn't have any money, so I turned to my sister Snezana for help, who lived and worked in Vienna. She immediately offered to send me $350 every month. *Great*, I thought. I would have enough to pay the rent, but I didn't know how I would manage to live on $170 per month. September came, but no one from the campus management asked for the rent. It worked for me. It crossed my mind that I might save some money. October came, and they did not ask for the rent either, but one day, they notified us that we could no longer live on campus and that we had to find another accommodation. The notification was addressed to all the Serbians living on the campus. We didn't speak Hungarian, and we didn't have enough money. In this unenviable condition, it was hard to find accommodation. We asked around at many places, but the moment they heard we were from Serbia, they did not want to rent us either a room or an apartment. The eviction day was getting closer. We were completely desperate when Andras Ambrus and his wife Ilona from church lent a helping hand to us. They offered us accommodation in Europrofil, the company they owned. If it hadn't been for their kindness, who knows where we would have ended up. We moved in November. We all had rooms on the same floor, and we shared the bathroom. My roommate was Paul, and Daryl moved here with his family as well. Jen lived there with her son, and her husband occasionally came from Serbia to visit them. We did the cleaning, taking turns, and thus, we kept the whole place tidy.

It took us a few weeks to feel at home in the new place. It was already mid-December when we started making plans for New Year's Eve. As we had a lot of space, we agreed to organize a New Year's Eve party in Europrofil. We asked Andras, the owner of the company, for permission to invite our friends to the party. He didn't mind, so he gave us his consent. Dragana and Zoran Meseldzija told me they would come with their children. I called my friend Sandor, his wife, Silvia, and his mother-in-law in Vienna. They were curious to know what our plans for New Year's Eve were. When they heard what we were planning, they asked if they could join us. "That would be great!" I said. I was delighted at the thought of starting a new year in the company of my friends. On December 31, my friends came from Vienna by car. In the meantime, Zoran and I went shopping for presents for all our friends. On our way back, we saw a vendor standing on the main square who had some Christmas decorations which he hadn't sold, so we bought them from him at a very good price. Loaded down with presents and Christmas decorations, we arrived at Europrofil, where Dragana was waiting for us with her two daughters, Anja and Andrea. There were also some other children there, and together, in the holiday spirit, we decorated the place. The party was held in the company cafeteria as it was the largest and most appropriate room. We put the tables together and arranged the food and drinks we prepared on the tables so that everyone could help themselves. Dragana and Zoran wrapped the presents we had bought in decorative paper and put name labels on them. Labeling the presents, we realized that Zoran and I had bought presents for everyone except for the three of us. We couldn't help laughing. It was important for us to show love and appreciation to our friends. I think giving matters. As the Bible says in Acts 20:35, "It is more blessed to give than to receive." We had a great time that night. Everyone was in a party mood. We were singing, joking, and laughing when at midnight, my roommate Paul dressed in a costume ushered in the new year by giving us presents and opened our hearts to the holiday spirit. The party went on until the early morning. Afterward, as there were some spare rooms, we offered our guests to spend the night there.

The next day, after a good night's sleep, Zoran, Paul, and I took our guests on a quick sightseeing tour of Budapest. They insisted on taking us to lunch to show their gratitude. We went to one of the restaurants on Vaci Street in the city center. Vaci Street is one of the world's most attractive pedestrian streets with lots of shops, souvenir stores, hotels, restaurants, and cafés with delicious pastries. After lunch, we returned to Europrofil, where we said goodbye to our friends, and they left for Vienna. I was glad to have seen them and even more pleased that they had a good time in Budapest. A nice companionship and festivities came to an end, and Dragana and Zoran had to return to their duties. From January 1, they were engaged in a project for a children's magazine, preparing a historical and geographical atlas of Hungary.

The new year was a fresh start for me. In February, I got a job at Eurorprofil. At the beginning of March, I met an American Adventist who was dating a Serbian girl. I was curious to hear how they had met. The American man told me that there was a Christian website, which helped Adventists from all over the world to meet each other. That sounded like a good idea. I went to Zoran right away and asked him to check out the website. Indeed, it was an Adventist dating site for meeting and connecting with other Adventists, but there were people of other religions as well. The membership fee was $20. I didn't have enough money. Luckily for me, there was a promotional offer of a seven-day free trial membership. *Great*, I thought, *I'll try my luck at finding my soul mate within seven days.* There were a lot of women on this site. Many of them wrote to me, and I responded, but Gabriella, a Hungarian Adventist living in Massachusetts, in the USA, caught my attention right away. Her first message was in Hungarian, which I didn't understand. That was the first problem. I asked my Hungarian colleague to translate it for me. Gabriella was interested in corresponding with me in order to get to know me better. *We've overcome the first obstacle*, I thought. Another problem was that I did not speak any English at the time. Since I wanted to present myself in the best possible way, I asked Zoran for help. We made a plan—I would write e-mails in Serbian, Zoran would translate them into English, and thus, I would communicate with Gabriella. I remember having to answer what my intentions were. I honestly wrote to her. I wrote that I was a Christian, coming from Serbia and that I wanted to meet a woman whom I would spend my whole life with.

I wanted to introduce myself to Gabriella as a man who had serious intentions and not just some adventurer. And I think she liked it. I asked her to send me a photo of her. She sent it with her next e-mail. Here is that photo.

Our correspondence became more frequent, and we were getting to know each other better day by day. It seemed to me that she was the woman I had been waiting for all my life. I had this photo taken with Andrea, Dragana, and Zoran's daughter, and I sent it to Gabriella. She really liked the photo, and she was glad to see that I loved children.

In Europrofil, I was responsible for cleaning and repairing used copy machines. The dust from the old toner cartridges was everywhere, sticking to my clothes, hair, and skin. Despite the safety clothing I wore, it was hard to protect myself, and it was impossible not to inhale the dust. All of us who lived on the company premises also helped with unloading trucks with appliances. These were mostly TV sets, washing machines, and copy machines. On Saturdays, I went to church. On Sundays, I didn't work, and every day,

I corresponded with Gabriella. Every day after work, I traveled an hour to Zoran and Dragana's place to read Gabriella's e-mails.

I eagerly awaited her e-mails. Every day, I couldn't wait to finish work so that I could exchange a few words with Gabriella with a little help from my friends. The more we communicated, the more sincere and emotional we became in our relationship. In one of her e-mails, Gabriella asked for my phone number. I thought about her all the time. I wondered what Gabriella from Massachusetts was really like, whether she was as adorable in real life as she was in her e-mails. What is the smell of her hair? What is the taste of her lips? What does it sound like when Gabriella from Massachusetts says, "Good morning?" I couldn't stop thinking about her. All these things and a lot more I wanted to know about her. And now when she asked for my phone number, I was scared. How could I tell her something straight from the heart when I couldn't speak English? At first, I somehow avoided giving her my phone number, but Gabriella kept asking for it. The next time she asked me, I wrote that it was not convenient at that moment and that I would send it to her later, but she did not buy it. I had to give in and send her my phone number. Still, I did not expect to hear from her anytime soon. But as a Jewish proverb said, "Man plans, God laughs." It was an irony of fate.

One day, I stayed over at Zoran and Dragana's place. Sometime around midnight, my phone rang. It was a call from an unknown number. I wondered who was calling. I hesitated for a moment before I answered. "Hello, Denis, it's Gabriella!" I was surprised and shocked. I was lost for words. It was Gabriella's sweet, angelic voice. She kept repeating, "Denis, it's Gabriella! Denis, it's Gabriella!" I did not know what to say. I was silent. As I did not speak any English, I mumbled something like, "Gabriella, I love you" in several languages. I didn't know how these words came out of my mouth. But they were from the bottom of my heart. They were pure emotions, unfiltered. Then we got disconnected. *Oh my God, what have I done!* I thought. I must have scared her off with my confession of love, and she hung up. Needless to say, I couldn't sleep that night. How long the hours of that night seemed to me! I was only hoping that she wasn't angry with me. I was impatiently waiting for the morning to check if she had sent an e-mail. These thoughts ran over and over in my head all night, and who knows how many times I went over our short conversation. At some moments, I thought that everything would be all right. It was just a little misunderstanding, and then I would sink into deep despair, thinking that everything was ruined, and she would never call me again.

The morning came. As soon as I heard that Zoran was awake, I jumped out of bed and turned on the computer. I washed my face, brushed my teeth, and sat at the computer, waiting for it to start up in order to check my mail. A little sign flashed on the screen, showing that I had a message from Massachusetts. I did not know whether to smile or cry. It depended on what was written in the e-mail. I dragged Zoran to the computer to translate the e-mail for me. I felt an incredible sense of relief or, as they would say in my homeland, "a stone fell off my heart" when I read the e-mail. As a professor of English as a second language, in her e-mail, Gabriella showed a lot of patience and understanding for my Tarzan English, as I would call my poor knowledge of the language. I was grateful for this quality of hers.

Zoran and I spent that weekend in church with other Adventists. Then on Monday after work, I hurried to see Dragana and Zoran again to read my new e-mails and reply. There was a surprise waiting for me. Gabriella wrote that she was coming to Budapest soon and that we would finally meet each other in person. When in Budapest, Gabriella usually stayed at her mother's condominium. Her sister, brother-in-law, and nephew lived in Budapest as well. We continued to communicate in the usual way. After work, I would always go to Dragana and Zoran's to read Gabriella's messages. I replied to her in Serbian, and my dear friend Zoran translated for me. He would always say that his English was not particularly good, but Gabriella and I helped his English improve by our correspondence. Over time, our messages started to look like love letters. I was impatiently waiting for June 22 for Gabriella's arrival in Hungary. Her family was going to meet her at the airport. She was planning to spend the first day with them while the two of us arranged a date for the next day at the Citadel, a famous attraction in Budapest.

I wanted to take pictures of our first date, so I talked to Zoran about it. I was too embarrassed to ask him for a favor to photograph us because only a few days had passed since his father had been buried, and he was preoccupied. But my friend realized how much I wanted the photos and offered to help me. We hatched a plot and got ready to carry it out. Since Gabriella did not know Zoran, his task was to act like some innocent bystander with a camera in his hands who would take pictures of us at the right moment. Gabriella called me several times that day. She got tied up at the hairdresser's and kept postponing our date. I couldn't wait to see her, but still, I was patient as I didn't want to rush her. The next time she called me to apologize for being late, I told her not to worry and to call me again when she finished. "I must see you today, Denis," she added in a half whisper.

We finally arranged the date for 2:30 p.m. Zoran and I arrived at the Citadel a little earlier. He situated himself a short distance from me, and I waited in great anticipation. When I saw Gabriella coming, my heart skipped a beat. She looked like just as I had imagined her—beautiful with bright, lively eyes and a smile that spread joy around her. I couldn't take my eyes off her as she was approaching me. I took a few steps forward to greet her. After that, we exchanged some small presents that we had prepared for each other. From the corner of my eye, I saw my friend taking some pictures of us. Then he rushed to have them developed as soon as possible. We stood there, chatting for a while, and then we took a leisurely stroll around the Citadel. We continued talking. Actually, Gabriella did most of the talking, and I just watched her and listened. She knew that I couldn't understand her, and I realized that it bothered her. I only knew a few words and phrases in English and tried my best to use them in our conversation. The whole situation seemed a little awkward, and at some point, Gabriella said, "We need to talk about us."

"I'm sorry," I replied. "I don't know enough English, but I know how to kiss you."

Gabriella smiled, our glances met, and I kissed her. Pleasure swept through me, and I kissed her again. We walked for a few more hours. She continued talking, and I was just listening and enjoying her beauty with my eyes.

Later that day, I took Gabriella to meet my friends Dragana and Zoran. They were delighted to see the two of us together. Dragana hugged Gabriella so warmly that she was confused. My friends were involved in our love story from the very beginning. I have already mentioned that Zoran was our translator. Sometimes, when he was not in the mood to translate my complex sentences full of emotions and gentle words, he would say, "Denis, this is too complicated. Why don't you write something simpler." And Dragana would usually add, "You can do it, Zoran! You can do it!" And so, thanks to my friends, Gabriella regularly received my compliments such as, "Your eyes are like deep lakes I would gladly dive right in."

It was a pleasant evening, and Gabriella felt comfortable with us. While she wasn't looking, Zoran handed some photos to me. As Gabriella was sitting next to me, she took a look at the pictures I was holding. "Denis, these people in the photos look like the two of us," she remarked.

"These two people don't just look like us. These two people in the photos are you and I," I explained.

"But how?" she asked.

We revealed the whole plan to her, explaining Zoran's role as an innocent bystander at the Citadel. Gabriella started laughing. "So you set me up!"

"Gabi, not only do I speak Tarzan English, but I am also as resourceful as Tarzan." We all burst into laughter at my remark. Gabriella liked my friends very much, and I was really glad about that. She immediately befriended Dragana, and I couldn't help photographing them together that night.

We stayed at Dragana and Zoran's till late that night. I had to catch the last bus to Europrofil, but Gabriella stayed a little longer as she was taking the subway an hour later. She enjoyed talking to my friends. She was glad they spoke some English. We made plans for the next day to go to the city pool.

I thought about Gabriella and our first date a lot that night. I hardly got any sleep. I was looking forward to seeing her again. In the morning, I called Gabriella and arranged to meet at the pool at 11:00 a.m. She was going to come with Dragana, Zoran, and their daughters, while I was going there with my

Serbian friends from Europrofil. Everything went as planned. When we arrived at the pool, I whispered to Dragana, "I'm not a good swimmer at all." Then I whispered the same to Gabriella. Dragana, as protective as she was by nature, warned the rest not to tease me about not being able to swim. Gabriella was gentle with me and offered to be my swimming coach. She took my hands and helped me float. Every time I started flailing around and breathing quickly, Gabriella would hold me tightly and tell me not to be scared. I really enjoyed my swimming lessons. It was nice to hold her hands and squeeze them tightly. She was constantly close to me. I could feel her body next to mine. Gabriella taught me how to swim for about twenty or thirty minutes, and then I got out of the pool, told her to pay attention to me, and headed straight for the diving board on the other side of the pool. "No!" Gabriella screamed. I jumped off the board, made a terrific splash into the water, and swam to Gabriella. "Well, well, you know how to swim," she said, directing a scolding smile at me.

"I have really enjoyed your swimming lessons. You are definitely a very good teacher since you have taught me how to swim so quickly." Needless to say, she did not believe a word of it, but we had a good laugh. We enjoyed ourselves at the pool the whole day.

There was a tennis court near the swimming pool, so we had some fun playing tennis too. There is a saying that time flies when you are in good company. It is true. We stayed at the pool until 6:00 p.m.

On the way back home, we stopped at the mall. When our friends left, Gabriella and I did some window-shopping. Earlier that day, Gabriella told me that she was planning to go to Lake Balaton on vacation with her family. I liked the idea very much. It was a chance to spend more time with Gabriella, so I asked her if I could join them. She agreed, adding that she had to check whether there would be a room for me there.

After I saw Gabriella home, I headed to my apartment, wondering what her mother would say about me accompanying them on their vacation. The next day, while I was at work, my phone rang around noon. It was Gabriella. She had good news for me. There was an available room for me at the vacation rental at Lake Balaton. As we were going on vacation in two days, Gabriella's family wanted to meet me. Thus, I was invited over for dinner that evening. Also, I had to convince my boss to let me take ten days off. Have I told you that my boss was a good man? He agreed to let me take a vacation. I was excited. I couldn't wait to see Gabriella and tell her the great news.

On the way to Gabriella's place, I thought about whether her family would like me. I also thought about what her mother was like. I was sure Gabriella took after her mother with her kindness. It took me a long time to get there from Europrofil. I had to transfer a few times, so I had enough time to gather my thoughts. Gabriella had a sister who was married and had a son named Daniel. I was eager to make a good first impression on her family to show that I was a decent man and that I cared about Gabriella.

On my friend's advice, I stopped by the florist and bought some flowers for Gabriella's mother. And there I was, a little bit nervous, standing outside the building with the bouquet of flowers in my hand. I rang the intercom, said my name, took a deep breath, and stepped in. Their condo was on the third floor. Gabriella welcomed me at the door with open arms and a big smile. When I saw her face, all my anxiety disappeared. I met Gabriella's mother, gave her the flowers, and got the impression that she was a nice person. Over dinner, we talked about how Gabriella and I had met, where I worked, and what my plans for the future were. As I did not speak much Hungarian and her mother did not speak much English, Gabriella translated the conversation for us. After dinner, we talked about our upcoming trip to Balaton. It was a very pleasant evening, and it turned out that I shouldn't have worried so much. At 9:00 p.m., I said goodbye and hurried home to Europrofil as at 10:00 p.m., the guard would lock the gate and let the dog off its leash. It was not a problem to enter the premises after that time, but then the guard would have to tie the dog up for me to get to the building safely. The guards were nice people, and I did not want to bother them.

The next day after work, I saw Gabriella again, and we discussed some details about our trip. We agreed that Gabriella's brother-in-law would drive her mother, sister, and nephew to Balaton as he had to return immediately to Budapest because of some business, while Gabriella and I would travel by train. Balaton is a lake, but because of its size, Hungarians call it the great Hungarian sea. This is a beautiful vacation spot. After a few hours of traveling comfortably, the two of us arrived at Balaton in the early afternoon. Once we settled in, Gabriella's family decided to go on a cruise on the lake. The boat was departing from a nearby dock.

This is a photo of Gabriella, her mother, her sister, and her nephew that I took before the cruise.

We stayed in Balatonboglár, a small town situated on the south shore of Lake Balaton. Our vacation rental was just 50 feet from the lake, so I took the opportunity to take some beautiful pictures of the lake.

The vacation rental itself was not large, although it included eight rooms and a well-equipped shared kitchen where we could cook food if needed. In the evenings, we ambled around downtown or along the beach, enjoying the red, orange, and purple sunset colors sparkling off of the lake. During the day, the sun was pouring down, but the evenings were pleasant. One of those evenings, I was told a family anecdote that every time Gabriella came to Balaton, she brought along rain and bad weather. So I promised them that since I was with them, the sun would not for a moment grow weary of shining. I also promised that the next day, I would make lunch for the whole family. They were a little skeptical of my promise. I suppose they thought that I didn't know how to cook. In the morning, after breakfast, they all went to the beach, and I stayed in to make lunch. I decided to cook Serbian bean soup. Serbians cook this dish more often with smoked meat or sausages, but Gabriella and I are vegetarian, so I made it without meat. And trust me, the vegetarian version is much better!

When the lunch was ready, I set the table and called my future in-laws. Obviously, they were very hungry as they came running and immediately sat down at the table. They helped themselves to the bean soup and salad as well, and I just sat there, waiting to see their reaction. They ate in silence for a while and then showered me with compliments for the delicious meal. I was pleased and relieved, and now I could help myself to a serving of the bean soup.

We spent the days at the beach, sunbathing, swimming, having fun, and doing different water sports. The evenings were reserved for pleasant walks, or we sat on the terrace of one of the restaurants by the lake, having a glass of juice or a piece of cake. We spent hours talking or simply enjoying the beauty and tranquility of the moonlit lake. I followed every step Gabriella took and every move she made. I watched the sunrays gently caressing her skin as she was getting into the water. I watched her loose hair with a sun-kissed glow that was like that of a fairy from a fairy tale. To me, she looked like a young birch swaying gently in the light breeze in the moonlight. Just as the birch is a symbol of spring awakening, so was she the symbol of love, happiness, and beauty awakening in me. It didn't take me long to fall in love with Gabriella.

Love develops in different ways. For some people, it evolves slowly and cautiously. They are barely aware of it until one day they wake up with a picture of their loved one in their mind—a picture without which they can take no further step. And yet, there are others in whose hearts the fire of love burst into flames like Chinese fireworks. With each passing day, I discovered something new and charming about her. I don't know exactly when, but during that summer, I realized that she had all the qualities I had always sought in a woman and that she was the one I wanted to spend the rest of my life with. I wanted to share my feelings, emotions, and happy and sad moments with her. I knew it was Gabriella who I wanted to create new magical moments and share my future with.

We had a wonderful time on our vacation. That was the reason why the days seemed to have passed quickly. In the blink of an eye, it was time to go home. We had great, sunny weather as well. It didn't rain at all, so it turned out that I had been a good weather forecaster. "You have falsely accused Gabriella. She can't be the cause of the bad weather," I said proudly. I could see they knew I was right, so they just remained quiet. Gabriella and I decided to take the train again, whereas Gabriella's brother-in-law came to pick up the others and our suitcases. After we paid for the vacation rental, we walked slowly to the train station. It was less than a mile away, and we spent most of the time talking about our life. We soon realized we were definitely cast in the same mold. Also, we both loved sports, and we felt the same way about our God. I remember Gabriella asking me, "Who is number one for you, me or God?"

I told her, "God comes first, but you are number one for me among people." She seemed pleased to hear that. We continued our conversation on the train. Gabriella suggested that I should take an English course when we got back home, and I agreed.

Hungary is a beautiful country with amazing countryside, and the train journey was pleasant, especially with Gabriella sitting next to me. When we arrived in Budapest, I stopped by Gabriella's condo. I didn't stay long as we were all tired after the journey. I said goodbye to all of them, but Gabriella insisted on seeing me off at the bus stop, which was near her place. I kissed her goodbye, but I didn't want to let go of her hand. When the bus arrived, it was time for me to leave. Although I knew I would see Gabriella the next day, it was not easy to say goodbye to her. We waved to each other until my bus disappeared into the distance, and she became a tiny speck on the horizon.

It was difficult for me to say goodbye to her that day. I said to myself, "If it is hard for me now, how would I feel when Gabriella would return to the USA?" The time passed very quickly. Gabriella spent two and a half months in Hungary, and during that time, we got to know each other better, fell in love, and developed a deep connection. And when it was time for her to leave, my heart was split in two. One half remained with me in Budapest, while the other half was getting ready to go along with Gabriella. On the last day of her stay, we went to see Dragana and Zoran to say goodbye to them. During those two and a half months, she became friends with them, and they became close to her heart. The following morning, I took a day off from work and booked a taxi so that Gabriella's mother and I could see Gabriella off. On the way to the airport, we were holding hands on the back seat while whispering the gentlest words to each other. Our hands were sweating, but we did not want to let go of each other. I wished our taxi would never stop. I wished our ride would last until the end of time. But taxi drivers choose the fastest way to get to their destination—they drive people and not their dreams, fantasies, or hopes. When we arrived at the Budapest Airport, our driver politely opened the door for us, got Gabriella's suitcases out of the trunk, and loaded them onto a luggage cart. Equally politely, he wished us good luck, a safe flight, and then he left. We went to the counter, and Gabriella checked in. We walked her to the gate, and there we had to let her go. I hugged her tightly one more time, and we kissed passionately. It was time for her to board the plane. Gabriella's mother and I stood on the airport observation deck, waving goodbye to our Gaby. We waved as she was boarding the plane. We waved as the plane was taxiing onto the runway for takeoff. We even waved when the Swiss Boeing looked just like a little bird in the sky. We wanted her to have that image of us waving from the deck, sending our love, care, and support for her. Lost in our thoughts and overwhelmed with sadness, Gabriella's mother and I took the bus from the airport. She went to see her other daughter Krisztina, and I spent a few hours wandering the streets aimlessly. I was wandering just to pass the time while my thoughts were with Gabriella somewhere high up in the sky, among the clouds. I was overtaken with an immense feeling of sadness and pain after Gabriella left. I lost track of time. It was already late afternoon, so I headed to my friends Dragana and Zoran. True friends are there to comfort you in sorrow and ease your pain, and the two of them were of that kind. I spent several hours talking to them, and it made me feel better. I was expecting Gabriella to call around 2:00 a.m. to let me know that she had arrived safely.

Unable to fall asleep, I was tossing and turning in bed, staring at the clock. I was thinking about how long it would take before I could see Gabriella again. August had just arrived, and she was planning to come again at the end of the year. Hardly had I dozed off when my phone rang. I looked at the clock, and it was just after 3:00 a.m. When I saw Gabriella's name on my phone's display, I was in seventh heaven. Gabriella arrived at her apartment in Massachusetts and called me right away. We talked for about half an hour, comforting each other, sharing feelings, and discussing the flight details. I felt calm after hearing her voice, but still, I could not fall asleep for a long time after we finished our conversation. It was not because of worries. It was because I needed this little happiness like the seed needs water to survive. Eventually, I fell asleep. I needed to rest to be ready for the next day.

I was very busy at that time. One day, while I was at work, my phone rang. It was my friend Jovan Iliev. Not only is he a good man and a good Christian, but also the author of numerous articles and books. In his book *Atheism versus Christianity*, he uncovers the delusions of atheism and evolution and proves the biblical truths. He expresses his opinion and gives the evidence, leaving little room for the readers to make their own conclusions. Jovan called me because he had a problem, and he needed my help. Early that morning, he arrived in Budapest from Serbia by bus, and he was flying to the US later that day. He was at the airport, but unfortunately, he had left his big bag full of books on the bus. He didn't know Budapest, and he didn't know what to do, so he called me for help. I promised that I would help him. Although I keep my promises, this time, the success of the mission did not depend solely on me. My boss, a good man as he was, let me get out of work early. It was a good start. I knew that there was a parking lot for buses with foreign license plates at the Chinese market, and there were always dozens of buses parking there. I didn't speak Hungarian. I couldn't get there quickly by public transportation, and I didn't know how I would find the right bus. Even if I managed to do everything, it seemed impossible that I could reach the airport before Jovan boarded the plane. However, when you have goodwill, perseverance, and a just cause, our God is always there to help us.

So let's go back to the beginning of the story. I was standing outside Europrofil, thinking what I should and could do when I saw one of my Hungarian colleagues. He was driving to the city center for business, so I stopped him. He didn't speak Serbian. I didn't speak Hungarian, so God knows how I managed to explain to him what my problem was. He told me that he had to go to the center right away, but somehow, I was able to convince him to give me a ride to the Chinese market and look for the bus. I don't know how we managed, but we found the right bus eventually. The driver didn't want to give me the bag, so I called Jovan to explain it to him. When I took Jovan's bag, I had to convince my busy colleague again to take me to the airport. He didn't want to do this first because he was already way behind his schedule, but God must have impressed upon his heart to continue to help me. Now we had to hand over the bag to Jovan as quickly as possible. My colleague was a skilled driver and knew the shortest and fastest routes. When we arrived at the airport, Jovan was just about to board the plane. He was anxiously waiting for me to give him his bag. I was running toward him like in a movie. The two flight attendants at the gate were very helpful and called the pilot to ask him to wait for Jovan. They were excited when they saw me. I made it just in time to give Jovan his bag. Finally, my mission was complete, and we were relieved. I am a man of my word, so every time I make a promise, with the help of God, I try to keep it.

I was very happy to be able to help my friend Jovan. He is a very good Christian, just like his sister, Snezana Iliev, a matchless benefactor. Snezana has helped many students graduate from the Faculty of Theology by providing significant financial assistance to them. She lived and worked in Germany at that time and spent most of her income on helping others. She also helped the poor, and via her sister Ljiljana and brother-in-law Pastor David Adamovic, she sent humanitarian aid to nursing homes and orphanages in Serbia. God has given the whole family spiritual gifts, and they live their lives selflessly in the service of the common good and God. I am glad that I know people like them.

When Gabriella returned to the US in August, we started talking about marriage. I introduced the topic by proposing to her one day. To my surprise, she hesitated and said, "We need to wait a little longer, Denis, and get to know each other better. We shouldn't rush into marriage. We need a sign from God that this would be the right decision." I knew it too, but I didn't expect she would hesitate so much. Also, there was an issue with immigration. Most people don't know how difficult it is to get an immigrant visa to the US. There are very strict rules about who can come to live in this country. One qualification is if you marry a US citizen. But Gabriella, at that time, was only a permanent resident and not a US citizen. This made it almost impossible for me to come to the US even if I married her. Gabriella had applied for citizenship in the previous year in October 1999. In April 2000, she had passed the citizenship test, but to her and her lawyer's surprise, she was not granted citizenship. This was very strange because when you pass the citizenship test, they let you know right there if you can become a citizen. They usually give you the date for your oath ceremony as well. But in this case, the immigration officer told her that they would notify her in two days. Her lawyer was perplexed by it. He had never seen anything like this in his career. Gabriella went home and waited for two days. But there was no news about her citizenship status in two days and not even in two months. Her lawyer did not know what to think about it. So when Gabriella spent two and a half months in Hungary that summer, she still did not know if she could become a citizen.

After she returned to the US in August, she decided to pray about it and ask God for a sign. She contacted her lawyer again, but the answer was the same. At the beginning of September, she called the lawyer to check on the status of her citizenship one more time. The lawyer called the immigration service on Friday, and there was no development. On Sabbath, Gabriella asked her Adventist friends to pray for a solution to this problem and for a sign from God if she should marry me. Without her citizenship, there was no point in getting married because I would not be able to come to the US to be with my wife. Gabriella and her friends from church prayed together that Sabbath morning that God would perform a miracle and give her a sign. When she went home after the church service, she was thrilled to find her citizenship acceptance letter in the mail. This was a true miracle since the day before when the lawyer inquired about her case, it was not yet decided. Overnight, the Lord solved the problem by a miracle. As this hurdle was overcome and as Gabriella became convinced of my honesty and love, she accepted my proposal. We informed her family about our plans and that we were going to get married at the end of the year in Budapest.

We started making preparations for the wedding. I asked my sister Gina to send me all the necessary documents from Serbia. The same was to be prepared for Gabriella. I went to the registry office with my future mother-in-law to book a date and time for our wedding. As you probably know how bureaucracies work, we had to fill out some forms. We also submitted all the required documents for verification and answered dozens of questions, but the registrar just raised her eyebrows and addressed my mother-in-law, shaking her head. I didn't understand what she was saying, but I realized something was wrong.

My mother-in-law turned to me and said, "Denis, chabar tu-tu-tu-rutu!"

"Sorry, I didn't quite hear what you said," the bewildered registrar replied.

"I was just talking to my son-in-law. In his jargon, this means that something is not going well," she tried to explain.

"Could you say that again, please?" the registrar asked, giggling.

"Chabar tu-tu-rutu!" my mother-in-law repeated with a smile.

"Okay, we'll settle this too," said the registrar, visibly heartened.

With great relief, my mother-in-law clarified the whole situation for me. Applying for a marriage certificate required Gabriella's presence and signature. Since Gabriella was in the US, we had a problem. But the registrar was willing to help us. She arranged our wedding on the condition that Gabriella would come to her office a few days before the wedding ceremony to sign the forms. We were relieved. Now we had to choose the date. I suggested December 24, but my mother-in-law reminded me that many people in Hungary celebrated Christmas Eve on that day, and therefore many of our guests would not come. "What about December 23?" I asked. She nodded. The registrar scheduled our civil marriage ceremony for December 23 at 4:30 p.m., and we carried on with our wedding preparations. We checked one of the tasks off our to-do list.

The next item on our list was to book the reception venue. Gabriella's mother, sister, and brother-in-law offered their help in finding the perfect venue for our wedding. We visited many restaurants and banquet halls but in vain. They were either booked or inadequate. When we almost ran out of ideas, some friends of ours told us to try at Hotel Budai. It is a nice family-run hotel on a hill, offering beautiful views of the city of Budapest. We were greeted by friendly staff, and the hotel manager told us they would be glad to host our wedding reception. We asked for vegetarian meals and nonalcoholic drinks for our guests. Most Seventh-day Adventists are vegetarian because we try to follow God's diet to keep our bodies healthy. Also, we do not consume any alcohol for the same reason. We were thrilled that the restaurant was able to accommodate us with vegetarian food and agreed not to serve any alcohol at the reception. This was a kind gesture from the owners because they heavily rely on selling alcohol at parties and weddings. After we agreed on all the details, we paid the deposit. Another important task was checked off our to-do list. Gabriella was speechless how well her mom and I organized everything for the wedding since I could not really communicate with her very well due to the language barrier.

Gabriella and I spoke on the phone every day. We discussed everything related to our wedding and rejoiced at each sign of progress. Gabriella wanted her sister to be her maid of honor, and I chose Zoran Meseldzija to be my best man. After we made the guest list, we started calling our closest friends and relatives. I called my sister Snezana first. She has always been my support, both emotional and financial, during the tough times in my life. I also invited other friends and relatives of mine. Thanks to Andras

Ambrus and his wife, they were able to provide accommodation for our guests in Europrofil. Marriage was one of God's first gifts to mankind, and Gabriella and I wanted to show my friends from Europrofil what a Christian wedding is like. Gabriella's mother told me to tell my friends to dance correctly. I asked her what she meant by it, and she said not to touch women. I assured her that this was not an issue for us because we did not want any dancing at our wedding. A wedding is a celebration of a man and a woman joining their lives together before God. It is a sacred ceremony sanctified by God, so we just played some Christian music in the background and enjoyed the food and the company of our relatives and friends.

Since the most important things for our wedding were done, I felt calm and peaceful and eagerly waited for Gabriella to come. It was December 15 when she arrived at the airport. In August, when I saw her off, she was my girlfriend, and now I welcomed her as my future wife. Our big day was just a week away. We needed to finalize a few things here and there, so we had to go to the registry office because Gabriella had to sign the forms. Gabriella bought her wedding dress in the US, and now we had to buy a wedding suit for me. I don't know how other grooms survive shopping, but to me, buying the suit was the hardest thing of all. Gabriella and I went to a lot of shops, and I tried on many suits before we found the one that fitted me perfectly. It might have been fun for someone else, but I was completely exhausted. We bought the suit, shoes, and accessories, and finally, everything was ready for our wedding.

The big day arrived. I wasn't nervous at all. The woman of my life was by my side. Our relatives and friends were also present, and the ceremony began. The town hall was filled to capacity with our guests. I had an interpreter on hand during the wedding ceremony conducted by a registrar. Finally, we were officially husband and wife. Cameras didn't miss a thing. All our guests congratulated us. After the civil ceremony, we went to the Adventist Church to get married in a religious ceremony. The service was conducted by Pastor Egervary Oszkar, and our special guest was my pastor from Serbia, Pastor David Adamovic. Everyone was cheerful. A friend of mine from Serbia joked that as we were posing for wedding pictures, I stepped on Gabriella's dress so that she could not run away. I did not mean to do this, but it was a good joke, and we all laughed about it.

After the service, we all went to Hotel Budai for the reception. Before the dinner started, I prayed to God and thanked Him for His blessings. With pleasant music by Michael Card, Secret Garden, John Tesh, and others, we had a wonderful time. At some point, the waiters brought some glasses and bottles of nonalcoholic champagne wrapped in linen towels. All the guests raised their glasses and toasted to Gabriella and me. I thanked God for His blessings, thanked all the guests for celebrating with us, and especially thanked Ambrus Andras and his family for their generosity. The food was amazing, and the service was fantastic. We complimented the chef and the serving staff. Even our nonvegetarian guests complimented the chef on the delicious meal. The reception was splendid, and everything went perfectly well. Together with our families and friends, Gabriella and I celebrated the beginning of a new chapter in our lives. I was happy to see Gabriella's friends there, especially her best friend from college, Andrea. Since that time, she has become my best friend too. Everyone wanted to capture some beautiful moments with us, so we took a lot of photos that day. Gabriella's sister and her husband, among other things, paid for a suite in the hotel, so after the reception, the two of us had a short two-day honeymoon.

A few days later, I applied for an immigrant visa at the US Embassy in Budapest. We had to have all our documents officially translated into English by an authorized translator before submitting them. On the scheduled date and time of our interview appointment, we went to the embassy. After reviewing our documents, a consular officer asked us a few questions. He asked us something like how Gabriella and I had met, how many people had attended our wedding ceremony, and other facts regarding our visits and correspondence. We also filled out some forms and showed our wedding photographs. There was no problem with our documents, except that I had to provide them with a police clearance certificate from Austria because I had lived in Austria for eight years. That was a problem.

Between 1987 and 1995, I lived and worked in Austria. I did not have a residence permit, just a tourist visa. This meant that every three months, I had to return to Serbia and then go back to Austria again. I got sick and tired of living in uncertainty, so when an Austrian man of Croatian descent offered me a solution, I accepted it without a second thought. He suggested that he set up a company and appoint me as its owner. That way, I would be eligible to apply for a residence permit. I needed to give him a power of attorney so that he could manage the company. I trusted him. I thought he was a good man and that it was a good deal. At first, everything was okay with our business arrangement, but things started to change. The actual owner started to delay payment to the employees, avoided paying taxes, and spent money on gambling. Eventually, the company went bankrupt, and I got a notice to appear in court in a few months. I did not know German, so I asked a friend to see a lawyer with me. When this friend saw the power of attorney I had signed, he pointed out that I could be in trouble. The lawyer told me the same thing. He also mentioned that he had heard of some bad Austrians who deceived foreigners the same way. I didn't know the severity of the problem. I didn't have money to stay in Austria, so I returned to Serbia in 1995.

Now that I applied for the police clearance certificate from Austria, they renewed the case from 1995. On the application form, I had to put down my address. This opened up a can of worms. The Austrian court sent the case to the Hungarian court to investigate. There was no way out. I had to hire a lawyer. I had to find a lawyer who spoke Serbian and hoped for the best. I explained everything in detail in court. I said that the man had deceived me and had taken advantage of my kindness. In the end, the judge asked me a couple of additional questions. He asked me if I was the company owner. I said yes but added that I believed this man would run the company legally. Then she asked me if my signature was on the company founding documents and on a power of attorney, and I said again, "Yes, it is, but I've been misled and deceived." The judge felt sorry for me because this Austrian man tricked me, but she had to send my statement back to the Austrian court. Now I was awaiting the final judgment. On the one hand, I was overwhelmed with anxiety about the judgment. On the other hand, I remembered God's wise counsel, "The truth shall make you free" (John 8:32). And this is true. If you believe in the Lord, everything will be fine. All I could do was pray and hope. For more than a year, my lawyer had no news from the Austrian court. I waited and waited, and it seemed as if everyone had forgotten about my case. It was very difficult for me that I had to wait and could not join my wife in the United States.

During that period, Gabriella came to Budapest to visit me every three months. This situation troubled us very much. Gabriella spent a lot of money on airline tickets. Her friends from the Adventist Church in Massachusetts prayed for us all the time. We were very thankful for that. But it was a very stressful time for us. My lawyer told me that I could face a prison term and a huge fine. We got very discouraged. So far, we had been praying to God to help me come to the US. We never asked God what He wanted with our lives. We just wanted our will be done. I even remember telling Gabriella that I would sit on a shark to ride across the ocean if I had to! Then, when we put everything in God's hands and trusted Him that He would work out the best for us, a miracle happened. Gabriella came to Hungary for spring school break. We decided to put an end to the problem. In a bit of despair, I asked a friend of mine, Sandor, if he could find a lawyer from Austria for us. He found an Adventist lawyer, and Gabriella and I called him immediately. Thank God the lawyer knew English, so Gabriella asked him if he could find out anything about my case. We gave him the case number, and he promised to inquire.

A few days later, on Friday night, Gabriella received an e-mail from the lawyer. We didn't want to read it. We were afraid to hear about the bad news. We just wanted to have a peaceful Sabbath. When we got home from church on Saturday evening, Gabriella asked me if I wanted to read the e-mail. I was petrified, so I said no. Gabriella went to the other room.

She opened the e-mail and started sobbing. I panicked. I went to see why she was crying. "I am crying tears of joy!" she replied. The e-mail said that a few months earlier, the Austrian court had exonerated me completely. Now we both cried with happiness. Later that evening, we called the lawyer to thank him for his help, and we asked him how much we should pay for his services. He said that we didn't owe him any money since he didn't do anything. He just inquired. We thanked him once again. It was a true miracle of God because I had been facing prison and a fine, and He just took care of everything. Eventually, the Lord gave us what we wanted when we put our trust in Him.

We stayed up late that night, talking and remembering all the things we had been through. We could finally be happy and realized that we almost reached the end of the road, but our happiness had cost us a lot. For eighteen months, I had waited for the certificate, and I couldn't go to the US to see my wife because of this bad guy who had deceived me and betrayed my trust. Did the Lord want to teach me not to be gullible and not to trust people easily? It might be. It was then that I learned that I should not trust anyone unconditionally. Trust must be earned. I trust God, my wife, my close family, and my friends. As for everyone else, I first make sure they are honest and truthful with me. We saw this waiting period as a test. Our marriage was put to the test from the very first day, but eventually, we came out even stronger and more in love than before. We spent Sunday walking around the city, enjoying the beautiful day with a feeling of peace and serenity in our hearts since we knew that our goal was there, within our reach.

The first thing we did on Monday was to call the Austrian Embassy and ask how to get the police certificate. It turned out that the only thing we had to do was to pay the fee, and we got the document in two hours. I could not believe that I was just a step away from going to the US and living under the same roof with my wife. Now that we had all the necessary documents, we literally ran to the US Embassy. Everything was in order, so I was granted a US immigrant visa right away. All my dreams, together with a lot of documents, were packed in a big brown envelope. I was supposed to show this envelope together with my passport when entering the United States. Since I had the visa problem taken care of, we went to buy a plane ticket for me. Gabriella was supposed to return to the US in a few days, and I had the ticket for May 11, 2002. Until then, I had enough time to settle some unfinished business in Budapest and pack my bags for the big jump across the ocean.

After we bought the ticket, we went to see Dragana and Zoran to tell them the good news. They were pleased and excited about my leaving for the US, but at the same time, they were sad that we would not be able to see each other so often anymore. They were and still are as close as family members to both Gabriella and me. There has always been this unique and unbreakable friendship between us. The unconditional love that I have for them and their daughters, Andrea and Anja, will remain the same forever.

There were two days left until Gabriella's journey to America. We spent them with her family. They were all happy to hear the joyous news that I would be joining Gabriella on May 11. This time, I felt a lot better than before seeing Gabriella off at the airport. I was sorry to see her leave, but I knew that we would be together again very soon.

My D-Day came. I was standing at the airport terminal, surrounded by my friends, waiting for the flight to Boston to be announced. I was ready to take the next big step in my life. On one side, there were my friends and in-laws with tears of happiness in their eyes, and on the other side were my new homeland and my love waiting for me to start our lives together and live happily ever after. Not only was it a four thousand-mile trip, but it was also a leap from one life to another. They say home is where your heart is. Mine was moving to Clinton, Massachusetts. While I was flying across the ocean, I remembered how I told Gabriella that I would come to her even if I had to ride that shark across the ocean. And now I was there, six thousand miles in the sky, and my biggest dream was about to come true. As soon as my flight landed in Boston, I was greeted with a warm welcome. Gabriella and her friends were waiting for me. I immediately felt better. The great big country, the United States of America, did not seem so strange to me anymore. I said hello to everyone and gave Gabriella lots of kisses and a big hug.

On the way home, Gabriella told me that her friends from the Adventist Church were throwing a welcome party for me that evening. It was a very nice gesture on their part. I freshened up after the long flight, changed clothes, and we went to the party. It was a fantastic party. The house was decorated with lots of American flags and other patriotic decorations. Everybody signed one big flag for me to remember my first day in the US. I still cherish that flag as a symbol of my new life with my new friends in America. I met a lot of new and interesting people from the Adventist Church. Finally, I was able to meet Gabriella's biggest emotional and spiritual supports, Angie and Ingrid, at the party. During our legal battle, they had been especially encouraging to Gabriella. Ingrid had given Gabriella $100 to help out with our legal expenses. She was a student at that time, so for her, $100 was a lot of money. I will never forget her generosity and compassion. I also would like to say thanks to Gabriella's friends, DeeDee and Audie, who hosted the party for us. I enjoyed talking to my new friends. My English was not so good at the time. I could understand people a little bit, but it was difficult for me to express myself in English. However, I am a talkative person by nature, so I managed myself quite well. We had a great time, but the tiredness started to take its toll on me, so Gabriella and I thanked her friends for the warm welcome and went home. I was tired and fell asleep quickly. I woke up in the middle of the night, and everything in the room seemed unfamiliar to me. I looked at Gabriella, who was sleeping peacefully next to me. I cuddled up to her and fell back asleep. Everything was all good finally. Marrying Gabriella was the best thing that ever happened to me. God never promises that all marriages will be happy, but if we follow His will, He will bless us and help us to have a happy marriage.

CPSIA information can be obtained
at www.ICGtesting.com
Printed in the USA
LVHW070430021021
699267LV00002B/2

9 781662 432347